DEVELOPING
CRITICAL SKILLS

INTERACTIVE EXERCISES FOR PRE-SERVICE TEACHERS

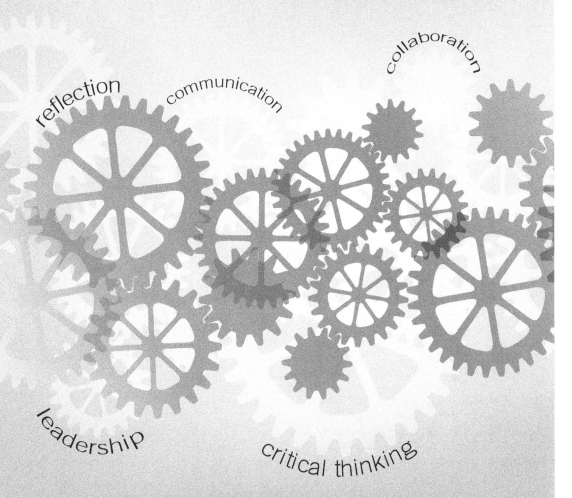

reflection communication collaboration

leadership critical thinking

Sally Ingles, Ph.D.

Kendall Hunt
publishing company

Kendall Hunt
p u b l i s h i n g   c o m p a n y

www.kendallhunt.com
Send all inquiries to:
4050 Westmark Drive
Dubuque, IA 52004-1840

Contents

About the Author

An experienced, certified public school teacher, Dr. Ingles taught at the elementary, middle school, and secondary levels before transitioning to higher education. While teaching undergraduate-level education courses in the School of Education at Spring Arbor University, Dr. Ingles's passion for measuring and developing candidates' dispositions and attributes was ignited. Her subsequent research was a validation study of a structured group interview used to measure teacher candidates' attributes and dispositions. A summation of that research study was recently published in the *Journal of Scholastic Inquiry: Education*.

Dr. Ingles's research on teacher candidate selection criteria also provided the foundation for the transformation of her institution's teacher candidate admission and induction processes. One of the hallmarks of the transformation was a newly developed induction course, "Critical Skills for Professional Educators," which replaced the "Introduction to Teaching" course. This professional development workbook is based upon Dr. Ingles's research and the related strategies she developed to shape candidates' skills and dispositions.

Dr. Ingles currently serves as the Dean of the School of Educational Leadership at Indiana Wesleyan University. In addition, she serves as a conference speaker and consultant on teacher candidate selection practices, sharing her research at regional and national conferences. Dr. Ingles travels across the country conducting workshops and training sessions for educator preparation providers who are seeking to implement research-based approaches to measuring teacher candidates' skills and dispositions at the time of admission.

Preface

If teacher educators can determine the disposition, knowledge, and skills of preservice teachers who are more likely to be successful in teaching, teacher education institutions and preservice teacher education candidates could maximize their limited time, money, and resources.

Fallon and Ackley (2003), p. 2

This workbook is not your ordinary education textbook—and I am not your ordinary author. I am an education faculty member like many of you, working diligently to do that which is right, just, and beneficial for our profession, our K-12 partners, and the teacher candidates we serve. *Developing Critical Skills* is a serendipitous culmination of my dissertation research, my experiences preparing preservice teachers, and the resources I created or collected while developing and teaching a "Critical Skills" course that replaced its predecessor, "Introduction to Teaching."

Perhaps, like me, you recognize the compelling need to rethink teacher candidate induction. We education faculty are keenly aware of the requisite standards, competencies, and dispositions to be met by those who aspire to teach. Identifying, developing, and refining those attributes in preservice teachers is a costly business. It devours hours, ravages resources, and matches our mettle.

And, yet, through it all, teaching and teacher preparation are among the most rewarding of vocations for those who are *well equipped* to succeed in the classroom. It is a labor of love for those who are called to inspire and shape lives.

But for candidates who are not well suited to teach and for the faculty who seek to prepare them, the induction process and professional development journey is fraught with frustration. It may ultimately end without certification or celebration. Such are tragic outcomes relative to the sizeable investments made by teacher candidates and institutions alike.

This should not be.

Ergo, this book was born.

The purpose of this workbook is threefold. First, it is to succinctly identify the essential skills and dispositions of an effective teacher. Second, it is to guide the development and refinement of candidates' essential skills and dispositions in an educational context. Finally, it is to facilitate student self-examination with regard to the most important question of all:

Are you equipped to teach?

Raising this all-important question early in the educator preparation program—long before student teaching—is right, just, and beneficial for all educational stakeholders.

I trust that this workbook will deliver precisely what it states and more: professional development for preservice teachers in the area of critical skills and dispositions.

To the learner considering a career in education, this workbook is a straightforward, simplistic introduction to the field.

To the teacher candidate preparing for more intensive field experiences or student teaching, it provides a refresher of the essential knowledge, skills, and dispositions of the effective teacher.

To the teacher candidate in need of additional support and remediation, this workbook is a valuable resource to be used in part or in whole to target to strengthen growth areas.

To the education faculty member, this workbook is a long-awaited resource that succinctly identifies the critical skills and dispositions of the effective teacher and guides the development thereof.

Acknowledgments

My husband and sons—providing unconditional support that enabled me to complete such a sizeable task

Dr. and Mrs. David McKenna and Dr. Pat Seraydarian—generously providing the McKenna Scholar Funds that empowered me to pursue this research project, present at national conferences, and publish this textbook

Kendall Hunt:

- Melissa Lavenz—seeing the value in the publication of this applied research
- Sara McGovern—offering patient, ongoing support through the publication process

Treasured Friends: Tara, Hills, Berlins, Grossers, and Moffitts—cheering and praying me through this project

My own teachers: Dr. Hamilton and Dr. Esterline—nurturing me as a preservice teacher and believing in me

Colleagues across the nation

- K-12 teachers and administrators in Okemos and Lakeview who inducted me into the profession
- Higher education colleagues across the country
  - Dr. Deborah Byrnes—introducing me to research-based group interviewing
  - Dr. Gillian Stewart-Wells—encouraging me to share this research with a broader audience
  - Dr. Kate Green, Magnificent Mentor—seeing the value in my dissertation research study
  - Dr. Vicki Luther—generously offering valuable insights at a moment's notice

Colleagues at SAU

- Carla Koontz—facilitating the transformation of this research into practice
- Ryan Donahue—endless design and formatting services at a moment's notice
- Jessica Pingle, editor and cheerleader extraordinaire
- Larry Pfaff, John Beck, Tovah Sheldon, Joan Fenton, Philippa Webb—for valuable contributions in your respective areas of expertise

My fantastic students over the past two decades; the student volunteers who participated in digital recordings

Above all, glory to God!

Introduction

If we genuinely want a highly qualified teacher in every classroom, we should not confuse a highly qualified taker of tests about teaching with a highly qualified classroom teacher.

Berliner (2005), p. 208

THE UNDERLYING RESEARCH

Contrary to conventional wisdom, raising cut scores on standardized tests does not automatically result in the selection of more qualified teacher education candidates. Even a perfunctory review of the literature indicates that standardized test scores, among other traditional admission criteria, are poor predictors of student's teaching performance. Dybdahl, Shaw, and Edwards (1997) concluded, "After more than a decade of teacher testing, research has failed to demonstrate any significant relationship between basic competency tests and . . . measures of program success, including success in teaching" (p. 252). Byrnes, Kiger, and Shechtman (2003) reached similar conclusions regarding GPA (Grade Point Average) and ACT (American College Testing) scores.

Findings such as these should not be interpreted as calls to abolish the use of such traditional academic admission criteria. Denner, Salzman, and Newsome (2001) observed, "traditional academic indicators themselves and the criteria applied, such as minimum scores, may have a certain degree of validity for predicting general academic success in teacher education programs" (p. 166). In fact, a case could be made for the usage of GPA and standardized tests as one measure of a candidate's content knowledge in any given content area (Petersen & Speaker, 1996). However, it would be a faulty assumption to presume that content area knowledge is predictive of teaching success (Zimpher & Howey, 1992).

A number of researchers have examined teacher candidates' verbal ability (oral communication and critical thinking), human interaction skills, and leadership skills during a structured group interview and have concluded that the skills and dispositions measured in that interview exert greater influence on teaching performance than GPA (Byrnes et al., 2003; Ingles, 2010; Shechtman, 1983; Shechtman, 1991; Shechtman & Godfried, 1993; Shechtman & Sansbury, 1989). This workbook is grounded in that body of research and keenly focused upon the development of those skills and related dispositions.

THE CHAPTERS

Chapter 1, "Precepts of Professionalism," introduces teaching as a profession and highlights the guiding principles and ethics of professional educators. Among the topics introduced in this chapter are principles and techniques for giving and receiving feedback, professional attire, professional introductions, and timeliness in professional correspondence.

Chapters 2, 3, 4, and 5, each identify, explain, and shape behaviors that are indicative of the four primary dimensions of teaching: "Oral Communication,""Interpersonal Skills,""Critical Thinking," and "Ethical Leadership." The guiding principles and practical exercises in each chapter will scaffold student growth and development in each of those respective areas. The exercises are not to be completed once and then crossed off in a "to do" list; they are to be completed both inside and outside of the class—in large groups, study groups, and "lab" times—until the student demonstrates proficiency and confidence in the respective areas.

Chapter 6, "Putting It All Together," can be viewed as the next level of rigor, for in that chapter students will be asked to demonstrate proficiency in the four preceding dimensions simultaneously—each in "practice" contexts that simulate a professional educator's practices.

In the first context, called Panel Discussion, the structure of the conversation mirrors building-level staff meetings, curriculum meetings, and professional development workshops. In those settings, educators must actively engage one another in a professional manner with adeptness within the aforementioned dimensions—or at least that is the ideal.

In the second context, the mock teacher interview, the student will be challenged to demonstrate proficiency in those same dimensions as when the spotlight shines solely on him or her. Teacher candidates will interview for numerous positions long before they earn certification, and early, proper preparation for these interviews may establish good habits.

The rationale behind Chapter 7 is that *all* educators must be competent in literacy skills. The focus of the chapter, however, is not an in-depth introduction to college writing or reading; instead, the focus is upon writing that educators most commonly undertake. From emails home to field trip letters, writing in the educational context serves to give students the nature and abundance of the writing professional educators complete on a regular basis.

In many ways, Chapter 8, "Professional Knowledge," can be used and viewed as a quick reference manual to educator-specific knowledge and skills. While oral communication, human interaction, critical thinking, and leadership are vital skills requisite in many service-oriented professions, the knowledge of and proficiency in certification standards, curriculum, lesson planning, assessment, and classroom management are quite uniquely entrenched in educator territory. Entire books and courses espouse the theory and practices related to each. The focus of this chapter is to provide nothing more than a "thumbnail sketch" of this educator-specific knowledge.

Chapter 9, "Field Observations and Reflections," is grounded in the theory that professional development is anchored in both academic training and apprenticeship. Presuming that many users of this text are just beginning an exploration of teaching as a career, this chapter provides the learners with guidance and focal points when observing in and reflecting upon the dynamics of pre-K-12 classrooms.

Chapter 10, "Dispositions and Documentation," makes a case for the presence of professional dispositions in the behaviors of an effective educator. Because shaping dispositions can become a time-consuming task, a faculty member must work smarter—not harder. Therefore, this chapter is a repository of documents to be used at the instructor's discretion. These administrative forms empower faculty members to efficiently and effectively communicate (and document) dispositional feedback to students, and—just as importantly—provide students the opportunity to self-report and reflect upon their habits of action and mind.

HOW TO USE THIS BOOK

Unlike a traditional textbook, you need *not* read it in chronological order. However, I do recommend that Chapters 1 and 10 are introduced early on in the semester so that learners are well informed—from the start—of the professional expectations placed upon them as preservice teachers.

But from that point forward, "jump around" as needed. Consider placing tabs at the start of each chapter so that the skills requiring the most attention can be addressed weekly or biweekly as needed. Use the practice exercises, peer assessments, and self-assessments repeatedly because growth, development, and habits are the product of practice and reflection.

Depending on the stage in the program when this workbook is introduced to preservice teachers, *Developing Critical Skills* may be used in different ways:

- To a newcomer exploring the teaching profession as a potential career, this workbook offers a simplistic introduction to the field.
- To the teacher candidate preparing for more intensive field experiences or student teaching, it provides a refresher of the essential knowledge, skills, and dispositions of the effective teacher.
- To the teacher candidate in need of remediation and reinforcement activities, this workbook is a valuable resource to be used in part or in whole.

To the teacher education faculty member, this workbook is a user-friendly resource that succinctly identifies the critical skills and dispositions of the effective teacher and provides ready-to-use activities, assessments, rubrics, and forms that will serve to develop critical skills and dispositions in preservice teachers.

FEATURE AND FORMAT AVAILABILITY

Developing Critical Skills will be available in print for those programs interested in a more traditional workbook with consumable, perforated pages. As students write out responses to "think and writes," self-assessments, peer assessments, and various other exercises, they will be able to remove those pages from the workbook and submit them as requested.

Developing Critical Skills will also be available as an eBook—downloadable to any personal electronic device of the student's choice. Instead of writing upon consumable perforated pages, the student will be able to type directly into the "writeable" documents as the documents appear on the screen.

The ancillary website, linked to demonstration videos for each of the primary skill-building exercises, will be available by access code for both print book and eBook purchases.

PRECEPTS OF PROFESSIONALISM

1
CHAPTER

I think the teaching profession contributes more to the future of our society than any other single profession.

John Wooden

Teaching is a profession. A noble profession. A challenging profession. A rewarding profession. A profession the ranks of which are filled with committed, well-educated, hardworking, passionate people who make a difference in the lives of the students, families, and communities they serve.

To join the ranks and earn the title of "Difference Maker," one must possess the knowledge, skills, and dispositions requisite of professional educators. The purpose of this text is to introduce you to these critical skills and dispositions while shaping your competencies in each of these target areas. In this particular lesson, we will focus upon the dispositions (habits of action and mind emanating from values and beliefs) of an effective teacher, and challenge you to begin your journey of self-reflection and professional development.

OBJECTIVES

The learner will:

- differentiate between *professional knowledge*, *skills*, and *dispositions*;
- examine the range of requisite professional knowledge, skills, and dispositions of an effective educator;
- reflect upon the *precepts of professionalism* in the context of teaching;
- self-assess current behaviors against the standards of professionalism listed in the "Precepts of Professionalism" document;
- develop familiarity with his or her School or College of Education's specific expectations for teacher education candidates; and
- evaluate his or her professional behaviors, skills, and dispositions to discern his or her readiness to enter the teacher education program and his or her "fit" within the teaching profession.

THINK AND WRITE

List three people that you have met whom you would consider to be professionals. Provide some general descriptors of the traits they possess (as opposed to their occupations) that led you to believe they are professionals.

KNOWLEDGE, SKILLS, AND DISPOSITIONS

Before examining the knowledge, skills, and dispositions of effective educators, it is important to first differentiate among the definitions of each. While professional knowledge refers to the wealth of information specific to the field (i.e., lesson planning, curriculum, assessment), skills refer to the abilities requisite to perform field-specific tasks (i.e., instruct, collaborate, lead). Dispositions are habits of action and mind anchored in values, attitudes, and beliefs (passion for children and content area, belief that all children have value and can learn, etc.). Dispositions are demonstrated through interactions with others (students, families, and colleagues) within the profession.

Because this lesson is intensely focused on precepts of professionalism, we will direct most of our attention toward dispositions of the effective teacher. In subsequent chapters, attention will shift toward the critical skills and professional knowledge of the effective teacher.

WEBCONNECT

Locate two journal articles, published within the last five years, that identify requisite professional knowledge, skills, and dispositions of an effective educator.

THINK AND WRITE

After reading the two journal articles mentioned above, prepare an abbreviated list of the knowledge, skills, and dispositions espoused by those authors.

 LET'S TALK

In small groups, compare the "general descriptors" of professionals you just composed with the list you compiled while reading the journal articles you located. Which skills and dispositions are common to both?

PRECEPTS OF PROFESSIONALISM

Undoubtedly, there are distinctive aspects of professionalism that are common across all professions (medicine, law, health services, and education, etc.) The following precepts certainly highlight that. However, they are explained in the context of the teaching profession. As you will notice upon careful review of the document that follows, the precepts of professionalism are predominately dispositional in nature, though skills are also intertwined.

EXERCISE

Carefully read the following "Precepts of Professionalism," and then develop a presentation (one of the following or a combination thereof) that will assist you in committing these precepts to memory:

- mnemonic device;
- hand gestures or body movements;

- poem, rap, or cheer; and
- visual representation.

You may complete this exercise with a partner or small group. Prepare to share your creative venture once the task is complete.

Precepts of Professionalism

Be a person of integrity—in both word and deed.

Make NO EXCUSES!

Attend faithfully and arrive early—*not* last minute.

Make NO EXCUSES!

Dress appropriately for the teaching situation: neat, clean, with proper hygiene.

Make NO EXCUSES!

Arrive properly prepared. Make NO EXCUSES!

***Be* present.** Not just physically present but *virtually* present as well.

Make NO EXCUSES!

Communicate carefully considering audience, *timing*, and *tone*.

Make NO EXCUSES!

Demonstrate courtesy and respect for others—even when it is not reciprocated.

Make NO EXCUSES!

Accept responsibility for your actions.

Make NO EXCUSES!

 **LET'S TALK**

Share your presentation with other groups. Provide positive feedback to each group regarding the most memorable portion(s) of their presentation.

Now that you have committed the precepts to memory, let us examine explanations and samples of the precepts individually.

Precept #1   Be a Person of Integrity—in Both Word and Deed.

Though we educators often state guidelines in the positive, this guideline seems to be most clearly expressed through a self-assessment of the contra indicators of acts of integrity. Take a moment to complete the following self-assessment. NOTE: In light of the fact that this is an exercise on "integrity," I implore you to tell the truth, the whole truth, and nothing but the truth.

Student's Name _____ Date _____

BEHAVIOR INDICATORS	FREQUENCY			
	Rarely/Never	Occasionally	Frequently	Always
I tell the truth, even when it may lead to unwanted consequences.				
I cheat on homework assignments.				
I cheat on quizzes.				
I cheat on tests.				
I follow through with commitments.				
I gossip (say things about others that I would not say if they were in the room).				
I say things to hurt other peoples' reputations.				
I steal.				
I lie if it benefits me or people I care about.				
I cheat only to help others who may fail without my help.				

LET'S TALK

How do you feel about your responses in the self-assessment? Would you be proud or ashamed to share this self-assessment with your professor or mentor? Explain.

 ## LET'S TALK

How would you feel if your favorite teacher's self-assessment on this chart was identical to yours? Would you be able to respect or hold in high regard a teacher who answered "frequently" to several of the contraindicators? Explain.

THINK AND WRITE

"Character is who you are. Reputation is what people say you are." As a burgeoning professional, which are you most concerned with? Explain.

Precept #2   Attend Faithfully and Arrive Early—*Not* Last Minute.

Have you ever witnessed a teacher pulling into the parking lot as students are entering the building? What message does that send to students? Have you thought about the impact of that tardiness on students? How about the impact on that teacher's colleagues?

 LET'S TALK

In small groups, answer the aforementioned questions. Brainstorm the many unintended negative consequences that ensue from this seemingly insignificant breech of professionalism.

Professional educators model excellent attendance, punctuality, and participation. In fact, their attendance and punctuality demonstrates a high level of commitment to their students and the teaching profession itself. Invariably, needs for absences arise on occasion. On such rare occasions, the professional gives his or her employer advanced notice—as opposed to a follow-up apology after the fact.

VIGNETTE

Early on in my teaching career in higher education, I encountered college students who balked at any sort of attendance policy or insistence that students attend class on time or early. "Professor Ingles," they lamented, "I'll be on time when it really matters – when I am a student teacher." If that had only come to fruition! Without exception, each of those learners exhibited the same behaviors during student teaching—with even greater negative consequences.

You may be wondering: What, exactly, is the point of this story? The point is this: Excellence is a process—not a destination. Excellence in all areas—including attendance and punctuality—begins now. Excuses should be left at the door. It is time now for preservice teachers to become today who they aspire to be as classroom teachers.

 LET'S TALK

"We make time for that which we value." With a partner, unpack that altruism in relation to teachers and preservice teachers with habits of poor attendance and/or chronic tardiness.

🖋 THINK AND WRITE

Write a response to the following assertion:

Chronic tardiness is the manifestation of selfishness. It is rooted in the underlying belief that the tardy person's time is more valuable than the time of the others who are left to wait.

Do you agree or disagree with this assertion? Explain.

Precept #3   Dress Appropriately for the Teaching Situation: Neat, Clean, with Proper Hygiene.

[This precept warrants its own lesson, and is explained with much greater depth in Lesson 5 of this chapter.]

Precept #4   Arrive Properly Prepared.

Professional educators are consistently well prepared. Whether they choose to forego valuable sleep time or miss out on appealing social events, professional educators meet their deadlines without making excuses. What is their secret to being properly prepared? Getting organized and staying organized.

According to Freiberg (2002), organizing is an essential skill for new teachers. In fact, Freiberg concluded that this skill is one of the most difficult skills for new teachers to develop proficiency. Effective educators do not miss meetings and do not miss deadlines because they have developed systems of organization that assist with managing time, filing papers, and keeping track of documents.

Some professionals even "file by piles." However, those educators who do so must be astute enough to place those piles where others do not see the piles and perceive them to be disorganized or disorderly.

📑 EXERCISE: "SYLLABUS SORTER"

One method a preservice teacher can use to develop a system of organization is to complete the "Syllabus Sorter" activity at the beginning of each semester. This exercise, which may require up to 2 hours, is one of the very best time investments you will make each semester. Complete the activity as described below:

Step 1: Gather all syllabi for courses in which you are enrolled this term.

Step 2: Select a calendar system for organizing all of the major due dates listed in each syllabus. Suggested calendars include—but are not limited to—Google calendar, a weekly print calendar, a month-at-glance calendar, etc.

Step 3: Enter the dates of all major papers and tests—from all syllabi—onto the calendar of your choice. You may choose to highlight or color code by class name or type of assignment (paper, test, quiz, etc.)

Step 4. Consider entering the pages of required reading on the Sunday preceding the week the reading is due.

Step 5. Complete the following chart:

Course Name	Attendance Policy	Late Work Policy	Submission Requirements (APA? MLA? Chicago?)
Example: EDU 100 Intro to Teaching	All unexcused absences result in a 25 pt. deduction in final grade.	No late work accepted.	APA format

Step 6. Make multiple copies of the chart and place it in several areas: class folders, on the wall by your bed, near your computer screen, etc. for easy access and repeated reference.

LET'S TALK

Which parts of the "Syllabus Sorter" activity were most cumbersome to you? Which were most valuable to you? What other features would you add?

 THINK AND WRITE

Share the parts of the "Syllabus Sorter" activity that produced the greatest benefit for you. Suggest one or two ways you could use portions of this activity to help your own students get organized and stay organized.

 LET'S TALK

On a scale of 1–10 (with one being the highest), how would you rate your level of organization on a typical day? Explain.

 LET'S TALK

Share with a partner one or two organizational strategies that seem to work best for you. Which strategies do you think should be taught to the students at your intended level of licensure? Explain.

EXERCISE: BEHAVIOR INDICATORS OF ORGANIZATION AND PROPER PREPARATION

Self-assess the personal behavior that indicates your level of organization and proper preparation.

BEHAVIOR INDICATORS	FREQUENCY			
	Rarely/Never	Occasionally	Frequently	Always
I start homework assignments earlier than the day before they are due.				
I meet homework deadlines.				
I meet deadlines set for me by others (employers, parents, etc.)				
My assignments show care and thoughtfulness.				
I arrive to class prepared with all materials and homework in hand.				
I arrive to work or practice (Music? Sports?) prepared.				
I follow directions without error.				
My presentations are well developed and create a favorable impression.				
I use a planner or calendar.				
I file my papers—even if by piles.				
I organize my room, and keep it organized (even if by distinct piles.)				

THINK AND WRITE

Reflect upon the results of the preceding self-assessment. How and to what extent does your current behavior align with this precept of professionalism? Explain.

Precept #5   *Be* Present. Not Just Physically Present but *Virtually* Present as Well.

It is not enough to be physically present but psychologically absent. Your attendance at a meeting does not always require your physical presence, but it *invariably* requires your intellectual presence.

LET'S TALK

Discuss the following questions with a partner:

Recall a time when you attempted to carry on a conversation with someone who was continuously texting or talking on their cell phone. How much of your verbal and nonverbal message did they glean? How did that make you feel?

📝 THINK AND WRITE

Should an educator's physical presence but intellectual absence be deemed attendance or absence? Should a student's physical presence but intellectual absence be deemed attendance or absence? Briefly summarize your positions on each.

Professionals are in the business of connecting with people. They are mindful that the person standing before them is their first priority and professional commitment. Because educators who demonstrate a high level of professionalism have the same view of class time and required staff meetings, they do not grade papers, tweet, or respond to nonurgent texts and e-mails at those times. Doing such things is not only discourteous, it is unprofessional.

Are there exceptions to this rule? I am aware of at least one. In buildings that are not equipped with intercoms and phones in each classroom, a teacher may need to keep a cell phone handy to respond to staff announcements and office requests during the day. If you are placed in that circumstance one day, your challenge will be to discipline yourself to avoid personal texts that may be received during the instructional day.

THINK AND WRITE

How often have you been physically present but intellectually absent as a student? How can you avoid that pitfall as you prepare today as the professional you aspire to be tomorrow?

Precept #6   Communicate Carefully Considering Audience, *Timing*, and Tone.

Have you ever experienced a time when your seemingly innocuous statement unleashed a fire storm of hostility from the listener? If that has happened to you, you may have already begun to discern that sometimes the problem is not caused by the words you choose, but rather by the tone and timing of the message.

Like Precept #3, this precept is rich with content. Due to the size of this critical precept, it is presented in much greater depth in the next lesson.

Precept #7   Demonstrate Courtesy and Respect for Others—Even When It Is Not Reciprocated.

Professional educators exhibit dispositions firmly anchored in the belief that *all* people are of equal value—deserving of respectful treatment. Manifestations of this deeply held belief include thoughtful, respectful speech, as well as acts of common courtesy. Such sentiments are only platitudes if educators abide by these guidelines only when they are treated respectfully. Consummate professionals know that respect must be shown to others even when respect and courtesy are not reciprocated. Specific strategies and guidelines for handling difficult situations are presented in subsequent lessons throughout this text.

Respectful speech is the cornerstone of respectful relationships. A dear friend of mine, a long-time pastor's wife, has often reminded me of the following three questions that serve as guides to respectful speech:

Question One | Is it true?

Question Two | Is it kind?

Question Three | Is it necessary?

These are valuable considerations for a preservice teacher, and they lay a solid foundation for conduct that is both courteous and respectful.

EXERCISE: "3 QUESTION TEST"—LEVEL ONE

With a partner, apply the previously mentioned questions as the "3 Questions Test" when evaluating each of the following scenarios:

Scenario 1.1

One of your friend's friends hangs out with your social group on occasion to watch movies and go to events together. Your friend's friend has a laugh that you find to be extremely obnoxious. Do you tell your friend about how you feel about this other person's laugh? Do you tell your friend's friend how you feel about her laugh?

Scenario 1.2

Your roommate plays music loudly and continuously—regardless of whether you are studying or sleeping. Your studies and sleep are suffering, and you feel you must leave your room to get any sleep and any work done. Do you tell your roommate how you are feeling? Do you tell others?

Scenario 1.3

You overhear a student that you do not know make disparaging remarks about your friend's personality. Do you tell your friend? Do you address the person who is making the remarks?

📝 THINK AND WRITE

What was most difficult about applying the "3 Questions Test" to the aforementioned scenarios?

📝 THINK AND WRITE

Is it possible to share information that may be hurtful in a kind manner? Explain.

EXERCISE: "3 QUESTION TEST"—LEVEL TWO

In small groups, apply the "3 Questions Test" to each of the following scenarios:

Scenario 2.1

Imagine that you are a classroom teacher who has permitted a small group of preservice teachers to observe in your classroom. As you are teaching a lesson to your first graders, the preservice teachers begin to whisper and giggle among themselves. Do you tell them to stop that behavior?

Scenario 2.2

Imagine that you are a classroom teacher who notices that one of your students regularly wears soiled clothing and smells badly. Do you tell the student? Do you tell the parents?

THINK AND WRITE

Compose a third scenario from the vantage point of the classroom teacher, and then share the scenario with a classmate.

THINK AND WRITE

Perhaps the greatest challenge in all of these situations is not *if* you say something, but *how* you say something. For one of the five previously discussed scenarios, write out a possible response you would share with the "offending" party.

 LET'S TALK

In addition to the standard use of "please," "thank you," "excuse me," etc., professional educators demonstrate hospitality to the students and families who enter their classrooms. In a small group, brainstorm what those hospitable acts might look like in a school setting.

Precept #8   Accept Responsibility for Your Actions.

Because we humans are imperfect beings who possess imperfect judgment and limited understanding, we occasionally make mistakes or inadvertently harm others. In those situations, we are posed with the following choices: apologize, deny, blame, or ignore.

Apologize:

Whether intentional or unintentional, our behaviors may have caused or contributed to someone else's harm. A simple "I'm sorry"—without qualifiers—is an apology.

Deny:

We can assert that there is no compelling evidence that our behaviors directly caused or contributed to someone else's harm. Therefore, we rebuff insinuations that we must apologize.

Blame:

We can point to others who contributed to the mistake/harm, and then insist it was their fault because the mistake/harm arose in their area of responsibility.

Ignore:

We can refuse to acknowledge that a mistake was made or harm was caused.

To be viewed as a credible professional in the field of education, the preservice teacher (and all teachers) must accept responsibility and take ownership of their actions. If those actions have harmed someone, the professional educator must apologize. A sincere apology—without qualifiers or excuses—is the best course of action for the ethical teacher.

LET'S TALK

Think of a time someone wronged you or made a mistake that adversely affected you. Did the offender apologize, ignore that it happened, blame others, or deny any personal responsibility for the act? How did that response make you feel?

THINK AND WRITE

You have read the author's opinion on this matter. Now share your own. Which of the four responses (apologize, ignore, deny, or blame) should professional educators use when they make mistakes? Give three solid reasons to support your position.

Professional educators demonstrate authenticity when they sincerely apologize for mistakes they make personally or for mistakes the school district or corporation may have made. Here are some possible ways of wording those apologies:

Examples:

"I'm sorry, Mrs. Smith. I forgot to send the note home with your son. May I get that note to you in another way?"

"Johnny, I forgot to tell the substitute teacher that you would need to leave early on Tuesday. I was mistaken, and I'm sorry. It is my fault that you were not dismissed on time that day."

"I'm sorry that your child's previous experiences in our after-school program have not been positive ones."

EXERCISE: "OWN IT"—LEVEL ONE

Directions to Instructors:

1. Ask each student to write out (on an index card) one accusatory statement that a parent or child may legitimately make to a classroom teacher.

   Examples:
   "You didn't tell me the test was tomorrow."
   "You don't even know my child's name yet."

2. Collect those index cards, shuffle them, and redistribute them to students.
3. Instruct each student to circulate around the room, randomly approaching individuals to read the accusation aloud.
4. During each encounter, one student will role-play the teacher and the other will role-play the accusing parent or accusing student.
5. For this round, the accused may choose to deny, ignore, or blame. The accuser may respond in a very natural fashion—not as a professional educator, but as a parent or child who has been wronged.

 ## LET'S TALK

In small groups, discuss how you felt as the teacher receiving the accusations. As the parent or child, how did you feel about the teacher's denying, blaming, or ignoring? What part of this role-playing exercise was most valuable to you, and why?

EXERCISE: "OWN IT"—LEVEL TWO

Conduct the exercise as you did at Level ONE, but this time the teacher (the accused) must practice taking ownership personally (or collectively on behalf of the school) for the legitimate accusations made. The goal of this Level TWO exercise is to develop and convey authentic, sincere apologies.

THINK AND WRITE

Which parts of these role-playing exercises were most valuable to you, and why? Suggest two ways you can begin practicing these behaviors prior to becoming a licensed teacher.

EXERCISE: SELF-ASSESS PRECEPTS OF PROFESSIONALISM IN YOUR CURRENT BEHAVIOR

Complete the following self-assessment:

Precepts of Professionalism	FREQUENCY			
	Rarely/Never	*Occasionally*	*Frequently*	*Always*
I behave as a person of integrity—in both word and deed.				
I attend class faithfully and arrive early—*not* last minute.				
I dress appropriately for the situation: neat, clean, with proper hygiene.				
I arrive properly prepared.				
I am both physically present and *virtually* present in class.				
I communicate carefully considering audience, *timing,* and *tone.*				
I demonstrate courtesy and respect for others—even when it is not reciprocated.				
I accept responsibility for actions— without making excuses.				

Perhaps one of the most critical dispositions of a professional educator that is not included in this list of dispositions is passion: passion for students and passion for content areas. Passion is not taught. Passion is not given. Passion emanates from the soul.

📝 THINK AND WRITE

Describe your top passions in life. Do children, adolescents, or content areas rise to the top of that list? Reflect upon your answers to these questions.

🌐 WEBCONNECT

Locate your School of Education's expectations for professional dispositions in its teacher education candidates.

🎤 LET'S TALK

In small groups or with a partner, begin sharing your initial thoughts regarding your level of readiness to enter your institution's teacher preparation program, and your personal "fit" within the teaching profession. Make specific reference to the "Precepts of Professionalism" and your program's professional standards for teacher education candidates.

EXERCISE

Reflect upon the results of your "Precepts of Professionalism" self-assessment. Compare those results against the professional behaviors, skills, and dispositions required of teacher education candidates in your institution's teacher preparation program. (You may also use the chart of Professional Skills and Dispositions included in Ch. 10.)

Compose a persuasive essay that makes specific references to the "Precepts of Professionalism" as you describe (1) your level of readiness to enter your institution's teacher preparation program and (2) your personal "fit" within the teaching profession.

GUIDELINES FOR PROFESSIONAL COMMUNICATION

1.2
CHAPTER

If wisdom's ways you would wisely seek, these five things observe with care:
of whom you speak, to whom you speak, how, when, and where.

The McGuffy Reader

Encapsulating the essence of professional communication practices in a single chapter is a daunting task. Nonetheless, it is an effort worthy of the undertaking, and in that spirit, I have compiled a "Spark Notes" version of Professional Communication Guidelines for the preservice teacher. Intermixed within these notes are practical exercises through which preservice teachers may refine their skills in these areas.

OBJECTIVES

The learner will:

- develop awareness of the essential guidelines that govern professional communication within the teaching profession;
- practice and refine oral and written responses to others that follow guidelines of professionalism;
- self-assess his or her adeptness at following guidelines of professionalism when communicating with others face to face and in writing; and
- reflect upon self-assessment and peer-assessment of practice performances.

The following guidelines for professional communication are categorized into three distinct areas:

Section A: General guidelines that govern both face-to-face and written interactions
Section B: Guidelines that specifically address written communication
Section C: Guidelines that specifically address face-to-face interactions

SECTION A—GUIDELINES FOR FACE-TO-FACE AND WRITTEN COMMUNICATION

A1. Clean and Appropriate Language

Though we educators often state guidelines in the positive, this guideline seems to be most clearly expressed through a self-assessment of the contra indicators of clean, appropriate speech. Take a moment to self-assess how frequently you use each of the following.

Student's Name _____ Date _____

PITFALLS TO AVOID	FREQUENCY OF USAGE		
	Occasional	*Frequent*	*Pervasive*
vulgar or profane speech			
racial, ethnic, gender slurs			
disparaging labels for any group (wealthy, poor, physically or mentally disabled, homeless, etc.)			
sexual innuendo, or related euphemisms of any kind			
nonstandard English			
slang for bathroom use (e.g., "gotta pee")			
slang for anger(e.g., "I'm p***** off")			
slang—in general (e.g., "butts kicked")			
jokes that include any of the above			

Even though you may choose to continue to employ some of the aforementioned language in your personal life, your professional reputation will suffer (and rightly so) for speaking in this manner in your professional life.

📝 THINK AND WRITE

Reflect upon your answers to the preceding self-assessment. Which of these pitfalls is the most pervasive in your language habits? Had you previously considered how these pitfalls will negatively influence others' perceptions of your character and status as a professional? Explain your answers.

📝 THINK AND WRITE

How and to what extent would you rate your current use of language as professional language? Use the aforementioned standards (or shall we say contra indicators?) when determining your level of professionalism in this area.

A2.   Appropriate Timing and Tone

Have you ever heard or said the following the phrase?: "It wasn't what she said, but how she said it." This observation speaks to the matter of tone. Whether sarcastic, insincere, impatient, or patronizing, the tone of a message is much more influential than the wording itself. Therefore, be on alert. Your tone *matters*, and your words as a preservice teacher can do great harm or even greater good—depending on the tone you use.

🖎 THINK AND WRITE

Read and then respond to the following poem:

> *"Come here!" I sharply said,*
> *And the child cowered and wept.*
> *"Come here," I said—He looked and smiled*
> *And straight to my lap he crept.*—Author Unknown

What emotions did this poem evoke in you? How could you use Guideline #2 and this poem to positively influence your career as a professional educator?

With regard to timing, this guideline is a weighty reminder that "It wasn't what she said, but it was when she said it." We educators must carefully consider not just *how* we deliver a message to our students and their families but also *when*. If a child or parent seems agitated, anxious, harried, or angry, these are not the most opportune times to provide constructive feedback. (With students, we may not always have the luxury to delay constructive feedback.)

With students' families or caregivers, we tend to have a bit more leeway as to timing. Mentioning constructive feedback casually when crossing paths is often not a good time to do so. Instead, when the constructive message is to be delivered by you, plan accordingly. Sometimes an educator's best approach to difficult conversations begins with, "I have been working with [insert child's name], and I've really appreciated her [insert compliment here]. I've also been thinking I should meet with you some time to get your feedback and advice on [child's name] and how we can collaborate on her [insert topic]. What time would work best for you?"

LET'S TALK

In small groups, share your initial reactions to the "timing" guideline. Which portion of the recommended advice will likely be the least difficult to implement into your professional life? Which will be the most difficult? Explain. In what ways could you begin practicing this behavior in your personal and academic life now?

A3.   Balanced and Fair Responses

The previous guideline stressed the importance of delivering constructive or difficult news in a manner that is sensitive to timing. But what shall we do in those instances in which we educators are the recipients of the not-so-positive feedback from parents, colleagues, or administrators? How do we respond as professionals (as opposed to individuals who have a wide range of temperaments)?

Regardless of personal temperament, professionals should not respond angrily, defensively, or in an otherwise imbalanced manner. Instead, we educators may need to excuse ourselves from situations in which we feel angry, criticized, or attacked. In a face-to-face conversation, we simply state that we would appreciate some time to consider the feedback before responding. We may offer to set up a time 24 hours later. By so doing, we will likely feel more balanced (less defensive) and more open to listening to the intent behind the message. (See Guideline #4 regarding suggested responses to attacking or accusatory e-mail messages.)

Regardless of how critical others may be of a professional, a professional learns to set aside personal feelings when making statements or decisions. Professionals: They do not attack others personally—even when they feel personally attacked.

See Chapter 1, Lesson 3 for specific guidelines and practice exercises related to unexpected criticism and role-playing of "The Confrontation" scenarios.

SECTION B—GUIDELINES FOR WRITTEN COMMUNICATION

B1.   Edit and Use Standard Conventions

This guideline appears to be rather self-explanatory, so let us move immediately to the related exercises on this topic.

LET'S TALK

After reading the two e-mails that follow, compare and contrast the level of professionalism between the two examples of written correspondence. Identify at least three improvements that must be made to Sample E-mail "A" to make it worthy of sending to a professional.

Sample E-mail "A"

hey. sorry i can't make it to class. i was up all night sick. let me know if i missed anything.

John

Sample E-mail "B"

Dr. Ingles:

I have not been feeling well, but I will make every effort to attend class. If I am unable to attend class today, I will make certain that my homework is e-mailed to you, and I will be certain to check my syllabus to prepare for the next class.

Sincerely,

John Smith

EDU428 sec. 3

THINK AND WRITE

Compose Sample E-Mail "C," which you could send to a professor informing him or her of a university-related absence that will cause you to miss his or her class that day. Be certain to avoid the pitfalls demonstrated in E-mail "A."

THINK AND WRITE

It is 10:00 on a Tuesday morning. The principal of your school just sent an announcement informing the faculty that he wants to have a meeting after school to discuss a fund-raiser. You have a dental appointment today at 4:00, which you scheduled six months ago, and because you have not given a 24 hour notice, you will have to pay for the visit whether you attend or not. Write an email to your principal explaining your situation.

When writing to an instructor or any other professional, it is also a measure of courtesy and professionalism that you include two critical components:

1. The recipient's name is listed in the "Greeting" (the opening line). Use a colon following the recipient's name if you have a formal, professional relationship with that person. Use a comma following the recipient's name if you have a more casual relationship with him or her. Examples follow:

Dr. Ingles: Dear Dr. Ingles,   Good morning, Dr. Ingles:

2. A specific descriptor in the subject line. By doing so, you have shown courtesy to the recipient regarding the matter to be discussed. This is helpful for the busy recipient who may need to treat the deluge of daily e-mail correspondence as triage. It is also helpful for searches at a later time when one or both of you wants to quickly review the e-mail conversation you shared on a specific subject. Examples follow:

"EDU 374 Lit. Review Question"   "Meeting @ 1 today?"   "reference letter request"

WEBCONNECT

Search the Internet for credible sources that offer rules of "Netiquette" (rules of etiquette when using electronic media).

THINK AND WRITE

Identify three rules of "Netiquette" that coincide well with the aforementioned standards of professional communication. Provide an example for each rule you list.

📝 THINK AND WRITE

Which of the aforementioned guidelines from Section B1 are "news to you"? In which ways must your professional correspondences with professors and other professionals improve in the days and weeks to come?

B2. Respond in a Timely Manner

A 24-hour "weekday window of response" is deemed standard and professional in many professional fields. Professional educators should be vigilant about responding to inquiries (e-mail, voicemail, etc.) within 24 hours on weekdays, and no later than 48 hours even on the busiest of weeks. If an e-mail is received on a Friday, the 24-hour clock does not "tick" between 5 p.m. on Friday and Monday morning at 8 a.m.

The 24-hour standard response time is unrealistic in the following circumstances: vacation, conference travel, illness, family emergency, etc. However, just because it is not expected that a professional reply to e-mails and voicemails in circumstances such as these, it is expected that the professional leaves "out of office" auto-replies or "out of office" voicemails so that others can anticipate the delayed response. An example of each follows.

Sample "Out of Office"—Voicemail

You have reached the voicemail of Mrs. Jones, fourth-grade teacher at Sunnyside Elementary. I will be out of the classroom on May 1st and 2nd. Your call is important to me, so please leave your name, number, and a brief message, and I will return your call upon my return. If you need immediate assistance, please call our main office at 555–1234.

Sample "Out of Office"—E-mail

Thank you for contacting me. I will be out of the classroom May 1 and 2 and will not be available to reply to your e-mail until I return on the May 3. If you have an urgent request, please contact our main office at 555–1234.

Did you notice that neither "out of office" response included an explanation of the reason for the absence? Disclosing personal reasons for absence is not necessary nor is it recommended.

LET'S TALK

Carefully reread the two sample out-of-office responses, and brainstorm a list of message contents that these responses have in common. For example, your list of commonalities could start like this:

1. Dates of absence were identified
2. _____
3. _____
4. _____

Suggest one or two additional pieces of information that would be helpful to the person who is calling or e-mailing the teacher who is not available:

1. _____
2. _____

✎ THINK AND WRITE

Imagine that you are a principal who is approached by a teacher who exclaims that he or she is just too busy to be bothered by leaving "out of office" replies on voicemail and e-mail. Compose a brief response that includes compelling reasons for that teacher to do so anyway.

Nonresponse Traps to Avoid

On occasion, you may receive inquiries from students, parents, administrators, or community members to which you *cannot* or *should not* reply immediately. Perhaps you are inclined toward avoidance, and you are tempted to disregard the inquiry altogether. For the professional educator, nonresponse is never acceptable. Following are FAQs and examples of appropriate responses in circumstances deemed *cannot* or *should not* respond immediately.

Q & A Regarding "Cannot Reply Immediately" Correspondence

Q: What are examples of circumstances in which one *cannot* reply immediately?

A: When someone has requested something for which you lack sufficient information to respond. (Either you must locate the information requested or await another's response to include in your reply.)

A: When you need additional think time before replying.

Q: How do I meet the "24-hour courtesy window" when I **cannot** respond immediately?

A: Reply within 24 hours to confirm that you received the inquiry and to state that you will need additional time to respond. Offer a tentative response date.

Examples of each follow:

> Mr. Jones,
>
> Thank you for writing. I anticipate gathering the information you requested by Thursday afternoon.
>
> Sincerely,
>
> Mrs. Ingles
>
> Government Teacher, Brookside High School

> Mrs. Adams,
>
> Thank you for offering to bring in your family's baby goats to show our kindergarteners. Would a Friday afternoon response allow you enough time to plan for the visit if we are able to accept your offer?
>
> Thank you,
>
> Mrs. Ingles
>
> Kindergarten Teacher, Sunnyside Elementary

 LET'S TALK

With a partner, brainstorm "cannot reply" e-mail circumstances that preservice teachers may encounter even before student teaching. (Perhaps in the context of professor/teacher communications? Inquiries from administrative offices on campus?)

📝 THINK AND WRITE

Compose a professionally written e-mail response to one of the "cannot reply circumstances" you and your partner devised.

Q & A Regarding "*Should Not* Reply Immediately" Correspondence

Q: What are examples of circumstances in which one ***should not*** reply immediately?

A: When the inquiry or communication elicits anger or frustration on your part.

A: When conflict is apparent and resolution is needed. (Do not attempt to resolve conflict via e-mail! E-mail battles tend to be LOSE–LOSE situations.)

A: When your mood is one which makes a firm, fair, or kind response unlikely. (If you are inclined to respond sarcastically, defensively, or flippantly, it is best that you wait before clicking reply.)

A: When the response necessitates a very carefully written, thorough, or particularly lengthy articulation (for which you do not have time within 24 hours).

A: When the previous "back and forth" discussion has grown unwieldy, or if significant miscommunication has arisen.

Examples of each follow:

Ms. Jones,

I am sorry to read of your frustration. Are you available to meet sometime this week so that we can discuss this matter further? I am available at the following times: _____. Please let me know which day and time works best for you.

Sincerely,

Mrs. Ingles

6th grade Language Arts Teacher, Midtown Middle School

Mr. Moxil,

Thank you for writing. I want you to know that your concerns are important to me, and that I will reply to each of those concerns as soon as possible. You should hear from me again no later than Wednesday. I am also available at the following times: _____ if you would prefer a face-to-face meeting or phone conversation.

Sincerely,

Mrs. Ingles

4th Grade Teacher, NotsworthElementary

(Imagine that you sense growing tension or misunderstanding between yourself and your cooperating teacher, administrator, or colleague.)

Mark,

Instead of continuing this e-mail exchange, would you mind meeting for coffee or after school sometime this week? I value our professional relationship and want to make certain that I am doing everything that I can to communicate effectively and avoid any future misunderstandings.

Thank you,

Shanna

LET'S TALK

With a partner, brainstorm "*should not* reply" e-mail circumstances that preservice teachers may encounter even before student teaching. (Perhaps in the context of professor/teacher communications? Inquiries from administrative offices on campus?)

📝 THINK AND WRITE

Compose a professionally written e-mail response to one of the "should not reply" circumstances you and your partner devised.

📝 THINK AND WRITE

Respond to the following quote: "For the professional educator, non-response is never acceptable." In two to three paragraphs, persuasively convince a reader to accept that presupposition.

SECTION C—GUIDELINES FOR FACE-TO-FACE COMMUNICATION

Though some of the previous sections of this chapter have exposed some of the negative circumstances in which we encounter educational stakeholders, this section directs your attention to the joy and excitement of encountering parents, colleagues, and community members for the first time.

First Time "Meet and Greets" with Colleagues and Community Members

Make eye contact with others when you encounter them in passing or upon entering a room. A simple hello or good morning is sufficient.

If you have not yet met this person, take the initiative to introduce yourself. Make a pleasant (if not smiling) facial expression, extend your hand as an invitation to shake, and state your position in the school if appropriate.

> "Hello. My name is Mrs. Ingles. I am _____."

Await his or her response. Example:

> "Hi. I'm Jack."

Respond courteously. Example:

> "It is a pleasure to meet you, _____. "

A handshake should be firm but not strong.

If the person has not disclosed his or her role at the school, simply initiate some pleasant "small talk" to break the ice and create a brief, pleasant verbal exchange. Close the brief conversation by reiterating, "It was a pleasure to meet you, _____," and then go about your business.

EXERCISE "MEET AND GREET"

Approach classmates in a confident manner, repeating the process described above. Learn the "dance" of giving and exchanging pleasantries during meet and greets.

🎤 LET'S TALK

In a small group, discuss your level of comfort completing the aforementioned exercise. What was least comfortable about the exercise? What benefits could you glean from that activity?

LET'S TALK

In a small group, discuss the role that the handshake played in the interactions. Explain how the handshakes that were limp or clenching affected you. Arrive at consensus on three important principles a preservice teacher must heed when introducing himself or herself to others in a professional manner.

Subsequent "Meet and Greets" with Colleagues and Community Members

It is entirely likely that you will have subsequent encounters with parents, colleagues, and other community members after your initial "Meet and Greet" conversation. In those passing encounters, make eye contact with those individuals when you pass near them or upon entering a room where they are. A simple "hello" or "good morning" is sufficient, and be certain to use names when possible. Depending on local standards of etiquette, it may also be appropriate to ask some version of the question, "How are you doing?"

Professional educators do not avoid eye contact, fail to acknowledge others in the room, or snarl (Did I grab your attention?) at others in their educational communities. The aforementioned guidelines will serve the preservice teacher well as he or she develops a professional presence.

 LET'S TALK

How and to what extent has technology affected this generation's ability to encounter one another appropriately face to face? How and to what extent will you teach your own students to encounter others using these standard practices?

✍ THINK AND WRITE

In two to three paragraphs, summarize your personal position on each of the aforementioned "Let's Talk" questions.

Traps to Avoid When Communicating with Caregivers

Even professional educators who are skilled at "Meet and Greets" may stumble if they are quick to make assumptions about the persons they encounter in school settings. To avoid making embarrassing assumptions when interacting with students' caregivers, consider adhering to the following guidelines:

1. **Do not verbalize your assumption of who this person may be in relation to the child.**
   Example:

   "Hi. Are you _____'s mother? Grandmother?"

2. **Instead, begin by introducing yourself.**
   Make a pleasant (if not smiling) facial expression, extend your hand as an invitation to shake, and state your name along with your relationship to the student.

   "Hello. My name is Mrs. Ingles. I am ____'s teacher."

3. **Await the caregiver's response.**
   If the caregiver does not reciprocate by introducing himself or herself, follow up with a polite inquiry.

   "What is your name? What is your relationship with _____?"

4. **Respond courteously.**
   "It is a pleasure to meet you, _____."

5. **Add a brief pleasantry regarding the child for whom they care.**
   "I enjoy having _____ in my classroom. He brings a smile into our room each day."

6. **Close the brief conversation** by reiterating, "It was a pleasure to meet you, _____."

 LET'S TALK

What if a caregiver does not respond as you would expect? Identify two to three possible explanations for that behavior.

Diversity Considerations

Even the most seasoned of educators will not possess awareness of all of the norms of every sub-culture that they may encounter during their teaching careers. Perhaps you will encounter a caregiver who avoids eye contact, does not shake your extended hand, or does not respond verbally to your question. Instead of assuming the parent is rude, aloof, or disinterested in making your acquaintance, withhold judgment. Follow up with a school counselor or other school personnel who have previously made contact with this caregiver. Your goal should be to partner with families. Seek ways to interact effectively and professionally in a culturally responsive manner.

 LET'S TALK

By what other professional means may you connect with this caregiver in the future? Generate some ideas with a partner and then record what you consider to be the best suggestions into the Think and Write that follows.

📝 THINK AND WRITE

By what other professional means may you connect with this caregiver in the future?

🌐 WEBCONNECT

Search the Internet for additional interpretations of what it means to "communicate professionally."

📝 THINK AND WRITE

Imagine that you are the author of this textbook, preparing a subsequent edition of this book. Which of your findings from your web search would you include in the next edition? Which guidelines would you reduce or remove? Explain.

1.3

Feedback is the breakfast of champions.

Ken Blanchard

Professional educators are in the business of giving and receiving feedback. As *givers* of feedback, teachers continuously provide feedback directly to students. Additionally, teachers then share that feedback with students' families so that students may grow and thrive academically, socially, and emotionally. As *recipients* of feedback, teachers continuously hear the perceptions, criticisms, and compliments from administrators, families, students, and colleagues.

The harsh reality of the "giving and receiving feedback" process is that it often makes people uncomfortable. Therefore, many avoid it altogether. For the preservice teacher, avoidance is not an option. In fact, a preservice teacher's level of discomfort with this process must wane so that he or she may thrive in an educational environment permeated by feedback. As the Ken Blanchard quote above suggests, the most successful teachers fuel themselves on the feedback that they receive.

OBJECTIVES

The learner will

- articulate the difference between *feedback* and *criticism;*
- self-assess knowledge of the basic tenets of giving and receiving feedback;
- explain the importance of giving and receiving feedback in an educational context;
- practice and refine skills in giving and receiving authentic feedback in a positive manner; and
- practice appropriate responses to unsolicited constructive feedback or criticism.

The words *feedback* and *criticism* are often used interchangeably. However, these words should not be used synonymously. While feedback is focused upon observation and reporting out observations without value judgments, criticism is linked to judgment and evaluation of the behaviors observed. Feedback can be positive (affirming), negative (disaffirming), or constructive (shared with the intent to encourage a different behavior in the future). In contrast, criticism is negative, often rooted in a spirit of condemnation without intent to encourage changed behavior.

To effectively engage in the giving and receiving of feedback, it is important that a preservice teacher takes on the "posture of a learner." This means that the preservice teacher must—in humility— seek first to understand before being understood; to be quick to listen and slow to speak; to consider that others' perceptions are valuable and important to one's growth and development. Such humility and openness will make the numerous self-assessments and peer-assessments (within every chapter of this book) fruitful experiences on the road to teacher licensure and successful teaching practices.

THINK AND WRITE

In your own words, describe the difference between feedback and criticism. Which do you prefer to receive? Which do you tend to give to others? Explain.

 **LET'S TALK**

In a small group, explain the importance of giving and receiving feedback in an educational context.

EXERCISE: QUIZ "GIVING AND RECEIVING FEEDBACK"

Complete the following quiz below.

Quiz: Giving and Receiving Feedback

Directions: Mark the following statements "True" or "False" in the space provided.

		True/False
1.	Most people say they would appreciate receiving feedback on performance.	
2.	Most people receive constructive (negative) feedback well.	
3.	Most people know *how to give* constructive (negative) feedback well.	
4.	Most people who perform below standards are not aware of it.	
5.	Most people improve after constructive feedback is given.	
6.	"Sooner is better" regarding giving constructive feedback.	
7.	Excellent managers give feedback constantly.	
8.	Denying people feedback is paramount to denying them the opportunity to grow and change.	
9.	Many managers avoid giving feedback so as to avoid confrontation and hurt feelings.	
10.	Many recipients of constructive feedback respond in a defensive manner.	
11.	Effective feedback is specific and nonpunitive.	
12.	Effective constructive feedback identifies what was wrong, why it was wrong, and what should be done differently in the future.	

Adapted from material developed by Dr. Lawrence Pfaff, Professor of Psychology, Spring Arbor University.

LET'S TALK

Compare your answers with a partner. Note: there are only three answers that are "False": numbers 2, 3, and 10. Which questions did you both get right? Which questions did you both get wrong?

THINK AND WRITE

What did you find most surprising? What meshes best with your past experiences? How will you apply this information to your development as a preservice teacher?

Now that we have established the need for providing feedback to others, how do we go about doing so effectively? Commit the following feedback tips to memory, and you will be empowered to give feedback like a pro:

"THE FEEDBACK FOUR"

1. **Get your "heart" right**. Start with the proper motive: to empower someone to be the best person they can be.
   Example: Can you—in good conscience—say that you are sharing information for the betterment of the individual as opposed to jealousy, a critical spirit, or even anger?

2. **Share observations only**. Do not share related value judgments.
   Example: "I noticed that you ended several sentences with the word 'okay.'"

3. **Be specific.**
   Example: "I appreciated your use of humor when you retold the cat story."

   Non-example: "Good job!" [This is both nonspecific and a value judgment.]

4. **Always give more positive feedback than constructive feedback.**
   Example: "I observed strong eye contact, meaningful gestures, and clear articulation. However, I also noticed that you ended several sentences with the word 'okay.' Despite that verbal filler, your use of humor kept me engaged the entire time."

Now is the time to apply these tips within a "Giving Feedback" strategy called "Sandwich Language."

To explain this feedback-sharing strategy, we need to examine the nutritional value of a typical American sandwich. Sandwiches are composed of three distinct parts: the top, the middle, and the bottom. The top and the bottom of the sandwich are bread, and in the United States, the bread used is often white bread that is made of a high content of sugar or sweeteners. (If you do not believe me, check out the label the next time you grab a loaf.) The middle layer is often meat.

If we use the American sandwich as a metaphor for giving and receiving feedback, consider that the first layer of feedback needs to be "sweet" (positive; the sugar), the second layer needs to be the meat (the constructive), and the last layer needs to be the "sweet" (positive; the sugar).

SHOW ME: "SANDWICH LANGUAGE"

View samples of an instructor and students giving and receiving feedback using sandwich language.

EXERCISE: SANDWICH LANGUAGE

[Script to be read by the instructor to the class following a viewing of the "Sandwich Language" video clip]:

"Just like a sandwich made with sugary white bread, we will provide feedback to one another in the order that a sandwich is assembled:

- Start with positive feedback
- Insert constructive feedback
- Close with positive feedback

And, as always, make certain that there is more positive than negative feedback so that the listener is not overwhelmed with constructive feedback. For this exercise, you will provide feedback to one another based upon your respective "Meet and Greet" performances from the previous lesson. You may begin now.

LET'S TALK

Using a scale of 1–10, with 10 being high comfort, rate your feelings as a giver of feedback. Use the same scale to rate your feelings as a receiver of feedback. Share your responses with a partner, explaining why you chose each of those numbers.

THINK AND WRITE

Explain what you learned about yourself from the "Sandwich Language" exercise and the "comfort rating" self-assessment.

📝 THINK AND WRITE

Explain how giving and receiving constructive feedback on performance is preparing you for giving and receiving constructive feedback as a classroom teacher.

Unexpected Criticism

Sometimes, we educators are the recipients of unexpected criticism. As professionals, we must take the initiative to manage those situations appropriately so that they do not escalate into a confrontation or end in unresolved conflict.

THINK AND WRITE

Imagine for a moment that a parent approaches you before class begins and queries in an accusatory tone, "Why don't you like my child?" How do you respond? In three to five sentences, write out precisely what you would say in that moment.

LET'S TALK

To your partner, read aloud (verbatim) the response you have written to that imaginary parent. Use sandwich language to give one another feedback on the responses you share with one another.

Now that you have experienced the difficulty of managing unexpected criticism, let us review some tips that will guide you as you successfully manage future encounters of that nature. The following tips are named "De-escalating Dissent," because our goal as educators—even when feeling attacked—is to seek first to understand the negative feedback or criticism we may receive, and then resolve it to the best of our abilities.

"DE-ESCALATING DISSENT"

When faced with unexpected negative feedback or criticism, consider using the following steps to understand the root of the problem and address it in the most professional manner possible:

Step 1. **State your perceptions of the confronter's message and emotions.**

> Example: Mr. Smith, you appear to be angry about something that happened to your son in class today.

Step 2. **Affirm your common goals and values.**

> Example: Your child's [Safety? Academic performance? Well-being?] is also very important to me.

Step 3. **Assure the confronter that you would like to better understand his or her perspective on the matter.**

> Example: Mr. Smith, I am caught off guard by your comment and I would really like to develop a better understanding of what you mean by this comment.

Step 4. **Suggest a plan of action to address the confronter's concerns, giving choices when possible.**

> Example: Let's find a time when we can discuss this matter appropriately. Would you like to meet today after school or perhaps tomorrow during my planning period?

Step 5. [If the confronter's agitation escalates] **Calmly restate the plan of action and reiterate the choice of options.**

> Example: Mr. Smith, I can see that you are frustrated. Let's choose a more appropriate time to discuss this matter. I'd like to understand your perspective. Are you available to meet today after school or perhaps tomorrow during my planning period?

Though we likely will experience a physiological "mirror response" (agitation, anger, etc.) to the emotion pressed upon us, it is vital that we educators remain calm and in control. Consider using self-talk (silently; not aloud) if necessary to remain calm and nondefensive.

> Example: "Sally, you've just been verbally assaulted and you are not in the right frame of mind right now to respond graciously. Breathe deeply. Convey concern. Assure this confronter that you are interested in hearing him or her out at a time when you can truly listen and respond more thoughtfully."

📝 THINK AND WRITE

Compare your written response to the "Why don't you like my child?" accusation with the "De-Escalating Dissent" Tips provided above. How and to what extent did your response align with the tips? In light of the de-escalation tips, what would you need to change in your initial written response?

EXERCISE: "THE CONFRONTATION"

Place your chairs in groups of four. Take turns—in pairs—role-playing the role of "confronter" and "responder."

Prompt #1: "Your students are afraid to talk to you."

Prompt #2: "Why are you always picking on my child?"

For the pair that is not role-playing, play close attention to the responder's words and body language, and provide feedback to that response using the sandwich language strategy. Make certain that each person plays the role of confronter and the role of responder at least once.

🎙 LET'S TALK

Use the sandwich language strategy to provide feedback to one another's responses to the confronter.

✐ THINK AND WRITE

What did you learn about yourself as you attempted to de-escalate dissent using the prescribed tips? How will you continue to practice in this area to develop greater competence in this area of responding to negative feedback and/or criticism?

✐ THINK AND WRITE

What are the most valuable "take aways" from this lesson on Giving and Receiving Feedback? Identify and briefly explain 3–4.

CODE OF ETHICS

1.4
CHAPTER

Knowing what's right doesn't mean much unless you do what's right.

Theodore Roosevelt

In a previous lesson on professional dispositions, we noted that educators behave like professionals when they demonstrate integrity in both word and deed. Among a long list of dispositions related to personal integrity, it is important to emphasize that teachers who hope to be esteemed as professionals should not cheat, gossip, or slander. They should never harm children physically or emotionally. Teachers should follow a simple guiding principle: Do no harm.

Though teacher scandals still make headline news on occasion, these scandalous behaviors should not be the result of educators claiming ignorance on the matter of ethical standards. National associations and state governments have taken clear positions on standards of decency and ethical behavior for professional educators. The purpose of this lesson is to introduce preservice teachers to the codes of ethics that will govern the licensed teacher's behaviors.

OBJECTIVES

The learner will

- locate codes of ethics for teachers from state and national sources and
- analyze the ethical and professional codes of conduct for professional educators.

WEBCONNECT

Locate the Educator's Code of Ethics espoused by at least two of the following organizations:

National Education Association
Association of American Educators
one Specialized Professional Association (SPA) related to your major or minor

(NOTE: SPA stands for Special Professional Association. Some examples of SPAs include the Council for Exceptional Children and Music Teachers National Association)

🎙 LET'S TALK

In small groups, discuss the recurring themes that you noticed among the codes of ethics you located. How would you summarize these principles?

📝 THINK AND WRITE

In your own words, list the guiding principles of the codes of ethics espoused by national organizations of educators.

🌐 WEBCONNECT

Locate the Educator's Code of Ethics established by your state's Department of Education.

THINK AND WRITE

What are the guiding principles embedded in your state's Code of the Ethics for educators? Summarize those principles in your own words.

 LET'S TALK

In small groups, compare the guiding ethical principles found in your state's Department of Education website with the common guiding principles of national organizations of teachers. Once again, focus on the commonalities among those documents.

 WEBCONNECT

Conduct a web search using the qualifiers "teacher cheating" and "teacher scandals." Read at least one news story per theme you found (e.g., cheating scandals and sex scandals).

 LET'S TALK

Summarize the two news stories you read related to teacher scandals. With your partner, identify the ethical principle(s) that the teacher violated in each case.

THINK AND WRITE

List the ethical principles violated in two of the teacher scandal cases you discussed with your partner. Explain how the teacher's actions violated the related principle.

THINK AND WRITE

Would greater emphasis upon codes of ethics in teacher education programs reduce the number of teacher scandal incidents involving new teachers? State your position with two to three well-developed reasons to support your position.

PROFESSIONAL APPEARANCE AND DEMEANOR

1.5

CHAPTER

First impressions are powerful. . . . People make decisions based on physical presentation.

Morse, 2008

As a classroom teacher, I was permitted on occasion to wear jeans and "school spirit" gear for special days such as Homecoming or casual Friday events. What I began to notice was that on days I dressed casually, students were more inclined to resist the normal classroom routines and ask the question every teacher dreads to hear: "Do we have to do anything today?"

Does an educator's attire, tidiness, and overall hygiene influence others' perceptions of his or her professionalism, competence, and approachability? The answer is an emphatic "yes"! Rightly or wrongly, teachers and preservice teachers are being judged by appearance and behaviors every time they enter a school. In fact, many principals state that every time preservice teachers enter a school building, they are "interviewing" for a teaching position.

Invariably, physical appearances influence others' initial perceptions of us. Not only should a professional educator's appearance be neat, clean, and properly fitting, it needs to be appropriate for the setting and teaching situation. To unpack these guidelines for professional appearance, we will focus on one feature at a time: contemporary interpretations of proper attire, standards of neatness and cleanliness, and proper fit and modesty.

OBJECTIVES

The learner will:

- examine norms of professional appearance within the teaching profession;
- contemplate the influence of an educator's appearance upon student performance in the classroom and others' perception of the teacher's competence; and
- self-assess his or her current appearance in comparison with guidelines for professional attire, standards of neatness and cleanliness, and proper fit and modesty.

As delineated in Lesson One's "Precepts of Professionalism," professional educators dress appropriately for the teaching situation: neat, clean, and with proper hygiene. Let us examine the three guiding principles of maintaining a professional appearance.

GUIDING PRINCIPLE #1: PROPER ATTIRE

The "just rolled-out-of-bed" look is never appropriate for professional educators. Therefore, the "just rolled-out-of-bed" look is inappropriate for preservice teachers as well. Sweat pants, pajama bottoms, yoga pants, slippers, and ball caps are not suitable attire for students in professional development program.

In contrast, "business casual" is what many school districts set as the minimum standard for professional appearance of their teachers. Business casual attire precludes jeans, running shorts, tennis shoes, beach sandals, flip flops, and slides. Therefore, business casual is the standard for the preservice teacher—at least for field experiences and classroom observations. (It is left to the instructor's discretion as to whether business casual is also the standard for classroom attendance.)

WEBCONNECT

Search the web for descriptions of "business casual," "appropriate teaching attire," and "inappropriate teaching attire."

THINK AND WRITE

What additional information did your web search generate? In one to two paragraphs, summarize conventional wisdom on appropriate attire for professional educators.

LET'S TALK

Reflect upon your K–12 teachers' teaching attire. Was business casual the norm? With regard to the teachers who dressed better or worse than business casual, how did students respond?

 EXERCISE: FAQS—PROPER ATTIRE

Read and discuss the following FAQs with a partner. Then compose a third Q & A on this subtopic and record it in the "Think and Write" that follows.

Q: What should I do if I don't have professional attire?

A: Consider borrowing clothing from roommates or going to a thrift shop for extremely affordable clothing. You do not need an extensive collection of dress shirts and pants. Simply rotate your professional attire and keep it clean and pressed.

Q: Why must I dress in business casual if other teachers in the building do not?

A: These other teachers are not interviewing for a position in the building as you are. They are not enrolled in a professional development course as you are.

 THINK AND WRITE

Type in the additional Q & A that you composed with a partner during the previous exercise.

GUIDING PRINCIPLE #2: NEATNESS AND CLEANLINESS

A teacher's clothing should not be torn (even if that is trendy), wrinkled, or soiled.

Just as important as the clothing is the personal hygiene. Hair should be clean, trimmed, and styled. Body odors must be eliminated (or at least masked well). Teeth should be brushed. Coffee breath? Onion lunch? Aarggh. Consider the senses of the students and colleagues with whom you work closely.

📑 EXERCISE: FAQS—NEATNESS AND CLEANLINESS

Read and discuss the following FAQs with a partner. Then compose an additional Q & A on this subtopic and record it in the "Think and Write" that follows.

Q: Should I wear facial piercings in the K–12 classroom?

A: Perceptions of nonearlobe piercings in many communities are not exceedingly positive. Consider carefully if the risk of encountering administrators and parents who are not receptive of piercings is worth the benefit of your desire for self-expression.

📝 THINK AND WRITE

Type in the additional Q & A that you composed with a partner during the previous exercise.

LET'S TALK

GUIDING PRINCIPLE #3: PROPER FIT AND MODESTY

Teachers are constantly moving: kneeling, reaching, bending, and stretching. Movements such as these may expose skin in the front, rear, and midriff, and "too much skin" exposure is both unprofessional and a distraction to learners. Therefore, preservice teachers should avoid wearing tight-fitting clothing in general. Women should be careful to avoid wearing short tops and skirts, and dresses, shirts, or blouses with necklines below the collarbone. Each of these items of clothing invariably fails to pass the "Stretch Test."

 ## EXERCISE: "THE STRETCH TEST"

Choose a partner who will either digitally record your "Stretch Test" on a personal electronic device or will give you feedback as to how much skin is exposed during each step of the "test." Then, complete the following movements when dressed in clothing that you have worn to classrooms as an observer or as a student teacher:

1. Stretch for the ceiling with both hands in the air.
2. Bend over to pick up a paper off from the floor.
3. Kneel down beside a desk as though you are listening to a student who is seated there.

 ## LET'S TALK

Give your partner feedback on the suitability of their current attire if it were to be worn in a classroom teaching situation. What pieces of clothing seem most appropriate? Which pieces of clothing could be problematic? Explain why.

📑 EXERCISE: FAQS—PROPER FIT AND MODESTY

Read and discuss the following FAQs with a partner. Then compose an additional Q & A on this subtopic and record it in the "Think and Write" that follows.

Q: What is wrong with wearing contemporary styles that are deemed "immodest" by the standards in this text?

A: Consider whether you want to be known for your physique and/or figure, or for your qualities as an effective educator.

Q: Would your clothing attire meet the school dress code for students?

A: If your clothing does not meet the school's dress code, you should not wear it.

📝 THINK AND WRITE

Type in the additional Q & A that you composed with a partner during the previous exercise.

THINK AND WRITE

What did you learn about the suitability of your clothing for the professional teaching setting? What was most surprising? What accommodations will you need to make for your current wardrobe to make certain it is appropriate for teaching?

ORAL COMMUNICATION

2

CHAPTER

Communicate in such a way that your speech does not belie your education.

Sally Ingles

Effective teachers are effective communicators. Undoubtedly, teachers spend much of their instructional day engaged in oral communication with students, colleagues, and families. From explaining to questioning, to directing and retelling, teachers are wielders of words. Though communication skills *alone* are not predictive of a candidate's teaching performance, "having a certain level of verbal ability is obviously a necessary part of a teacher's vital skill set" (Andrew, Cobb, & Giampietro, 2005, p. 348).

Most teacher candidates enter teacher preparation programs with average or above-average verbal ability as measured by standardized test scores. However, these measures are not indicative of the candidate's *oral* speech patterns, speech fluency, and other related behaviors that comprise effective oral communication. Therefore, this chapter places an intensive focus on the development of teacher candidates' oral communication skills and the language they will ultimately "wield" as professional educators: educational jargon.

2.1
CHAPTER

VERBAL FILLERS

OBJECTIVES

The learner will:

- develop self-awareness of the most pervasive verbal fillers used in personal speech;
- self-assess proficiency in oral communication skills;
- refine oral communication skills by focusing upon the removal of verbal fillers; and
- reflect upon self-assessment and peer-assessment of practice performances.

VERBAL FILLERS

Throughout my tenure as professor of education, I have encountered a number of aspiring preservice teachers who have excitedly shared their reasons for pursuing a degree in education. Unfortunately, too often a student's expressed passion for teaching is obfuscated by the manner in which he or she speaks.

VIGNETTE 2.1

> *"Like . . . I . . . like . . . want to be . . . like . . . a teacher, because . . . like . . . I really love kids. I'm just . . . like . . . really good . . . like . . . with kids, ya know? They're . . . like . . . sooooo cute!"*

Many preservice teachers who use this speech pattern truly are passionate about teaching and helping children. How unfortunate that their passions are overshadowed by their difficulties in oral communication. The encouraging news in the midst of this message is that the usage of verbal fillers in oral speech is an addiction that has been shown to respond well to treatment if the speaker is willing to submit to three steps:

Step One | Admit he or she has a problem.
Step Two | Actively participate in intensive therapy (called Exercises) as prescribed by a course instructor.
Step Three | Submit to accountability.

All joking aside, I must admit that I know how it feels to be a recovering "addict," once addicted to the word "like." As an aspiring Language Arts teacher at the height of my improper usage of the English language, I came to the realization that I could not teach what I did not possess: articulate speech. The three-step intervention has served me well, and I am confident that the ensuing exercises repeated on an ongoing basis will significantly enhance your poise and speech patterns. I believe that you, too, can regain command of the English language so that your oral communication does not belie your professional education.

In Figure 2.1, you will notice a list of the most commonly spoken verbal fillers that I have noted over the past two decades. I have deemed them "infamous" because they have are looked upon with great disdain by lovers of the English language and professors-at-large.

Figure 2.1 Common Verbal Fillers

The "Infamous Eight"

umm
uhh
like/it's like
and . . . and . . . and . . .
ya know
okay
so
I mean

📝 THINK AND WRITE

How many times have you heard a friend or classmate use a speech pattern similar to the one noted at the beginning of the chapter? Consider for a moment how the sheer number of verbal fillers reduced the efficiency of the spoken word and threatened to overshadow the speaker's intended message. Explain your initial reaction to the "like . . . like . . ." speech pattern and its impact upon the speaker's efficiency and message.

📝 THINK AND WRITE

Imagine that your doctor, lawyer, or teacher, spoke in a similar manner—riddled with verbal fillers. What negative assumptions might you make about that professional based upon speech pattern alone?

EXERCISE

Take a moment to complete Self-Assessment 2.2. Place a check mark in the column that best describes how frequently you think you use each of the following verbal fillers:

Self-Assessment 2.2

Student's Name _____ Date _____

VERBAL FILLER	FREQUENCY OF USAGE		
	Occasional	*Frequent*	*Pervasive*
umm			
uhh			
like/it's like			
and . . . and . . . and . . .			
ya know			
okay			
so			
I mean			
PRONUNCIATION ERRORS	*Occasional*	*Frequent*	*Pervasive*
fur (for)			
tuh (to)			

THINK AND WRITE

Reflect upon your answers to the preceding self-assessment. Overall, do you believe that your speech is creating a favorable or an unfavorable impression of your intellect, education, and competence? Explain your answer.

SPEECH WITHOUT VERBAL FILLERS

Educated people develop proficiency with the English language. Years of reading, writing, and public speaking hone the educated person's communication skills. The product of such intensive work is articulate, clear, and fluent speech.

Because pervasive errors hamper communication and thwart a teacher's efforts to efficiently communicate with students and stakeholders, it is imperative that preservice teachers practice oral communication skills until verbal fillers dissipate.

Is there any single strategy that seems to work best for removing verbal fillers from speech? For starters, one must learn to embrace the silence. It is far better to pause for a moment of contemplation than to break that silence with verbal fillers. What may seem like an eternity to the speaker is often only a second or two of silence. If necessary, the speaker should simply inform the audience that some processing time is needed before responding to the question posed. It is preferable to embrace the silence instead of masking it.

Secondly, a speaker needs to practice being "put on the spot"—placed in the center of the room without a prepared script, so that with time he or she develops the poise and confidence to think and then speak while under pressure—without leaning on unnecessary words.

As we develop awareness of the verbal fillers that pervade our own speech and the speech of community members, we speakers and audience members may be tempted to become overly critical. "Calling out" one another's verbal fillers can be a sensitive area in the classroom. Therefore, it is vital that a supportive learning community is established. In safe learning communities, members encourage one another to stretch and take risks. When members fall short of the goal, they are to be encouraged and supported. Falling short of a goal is not failure. Refusal to keep trying is failure.

The following exercise is a lighthearted activity wherein students face their fears of public speaking in a fictitious context of serving as a "visiting professor." During this exercise, students are challenged to remove verbal fillers from their own speech patterns when they are chosen to speak in front of the group and to alert classmates of any undetected usage of verbal fillers when they play the role of audience member.

▶ SHOW ME: "UMM GAME"

View an instructor introducing the "Umm Game" exercise to students and her students' first attempts at speaking without verbal fillers.

Note to Instructors: As a general rule, the course instructor is the first "visiting professor" to complete the exercise. Thereafter, attempt to select only volunteers in the first few class periods, reminding students that ALL will be given the opportunity to showcase their skills in front of the entire group before the end of the semester. To generate a list of random topics for the "visiting professor" to discuss, simply ask students to generate random topics on index cards so that you have a "ready pool" of questions from which to draw.

EXERCISE: "UMM GAME"— LEVEL ONE ("Visiting Professor")

[Script to be read by the Instructor to the class following a viewing of the "Umm Game" video clip]:

"Class, we have a guest professor, visiting us from [the student volunteer chooses the name of the university]. Dr. [student's last name] will be sharing with us [his or her] research on [randomly assigned topic]". Dr. _____, you may begin now. . . . "

Over the course of the remaining 30 seconds, the speaker must address the assigned topic (completely fictitious content, usually) while refraining from the use of "umm," "uhh," "like," repeated usages of "and," and other forms of verbal fillers. If at any point the speaker uses verbal fillers, the class *immediately* claps politely—encouraging the speaker to start over. The "visiting professor" starts over, and the clock is reset for 30 seconds.

The "Umm Game"—after repeated modeling—should be practiced in small groups and eventually expanded to impromptu speeches in front of the entire class.

🎙 LET'S TALK

As you listen to a classmate play the "visiting professor" role in the "Umm Game," complete the Peer Assessment 2.3 table. Upon completion of the peer assessment, use the sandwich language strategy (presented in Chapter 1) while sharing constructive feedback to your classmate in a positive manner.

Peer Assessment 2.3

Student's Name _____ Date _____

VERBAL FILLER	FREQUENCY OF USAGE		
	Occasional	*Frequent*	*Pervasive*
umm			
uhh			
like/it's like			
and . . . and . . . and . . .			
ya know			
okay			
so			
I mean			
PRONUNCIATION ERRORS	*Occasional*	*Frequent*	*Pervasive*
fur (for)			
tuh (to)			

EXERCISE

Ask a classmate to use his or her iPad or SmartPhone to tape your subsequent attempts at "filler-free" speech. Then take a minute to review the recording and self-assess using the following chart.

Self-Assessment 2.4

Student's Name _____ Date _____

VERBAL FILLER	FREQUENCY OF USAGE		
	Occasional	*Frequent*	*Pervasive*
umm			
uhh			
like/it's like			
and . . . and . . . and . . .			
ya know			
okay			
so			
I mean			
PRONUNCIATION ERRORS	*Occasional*	*Frequent*	*Pervasive*
fur (for)			
tuh (to)			

THINK AND WRITE

Compare your first self-assessment (before attempting the "Umm Game") and your second self-assessment that followed.

Which verbal filler(s) are you most tempted to use?

How often do you hear yourself using that and other fillers? (all of the time, most of the time, some of the time, not very often)

Why do you think that is the case?

THINK AND WRITE

List two individuals you will ask to hold you accountable—to "call you out" when you begin relying upon verbal fillers. How exactly will these individuals alert you to improper usage of verbal fillers? Explain.

EXERCISE: "UMM GAME"—LEVEL TWO ("PERSUADE ME")

This stage should be a bit more challenging than the last, so make certain that you have practiced sufficiently at Level One before proceeding.

Instructions: The instructor will bring a collection of objects into the room or predetermine a list of objects already present in the room. Each student will be given the name of the object to be discussed, 10 seconds of "think time," and then he or she must persuade the audience of the object's practical use and/or value in an educational setting—all the while avoiding using verbal fillers.

During this level, however, students may not use fictitious responses. Plausible statements of an object's practical use and/or value in a classroom setting must be shared.

Examples:

- rectangular table (student workstation for larger groups; a station for classroom supplies, etc.) and
- popsicle sticks (inscribed with student names; to be drawn from a jar to determine next student participant).

[Script to be read by the Instructor]

"Class, we educators must be resourceful people considering limited budgets and various competing needs for those funds. Your classmate, [student's name], has devised a plan to make [name of object] of tremendous practical value to the classroom teacher. [Student Name], you may begin persuading us of the practical value of this object now...."

Over the course of the remaining 30 seconds, the speaker must address the assigned topic (both factual and persuasive) while refraining from the use of "umm," "uhh," "like," repeated usages of "and," and other forms of verbal fillers. If at any point the speaker uses verbal fillers, the class *immediately* claps politely—encouraging the speaker to start over. The student speaker is asked to start over, and the clock is reset for 30 seconds.

The "Umm Game"—after repeated modeling—should be practiced in small groups and eventually expanded to impromptu speeches in front of the entire class.

 LET'S TALK

As you listen to a classmate speak in the "Persuade Me" role of the "Umm Game"—Level TWO, complete the Peer Assessment 2.3 table. Upon completion of the peer assessment, use the sandwich language strategy (presented in Chapter 1) while sharing constructive feedback to your classmate in a positive manner.

Peer Assessment 2.5

Student's Name _____ Date _____

Behavior Indicators: Oral Communication

	ACCEPTABLE	**NEEDS IMPROVEMENT**
Use of verbal fillers	Free of verbal fillers; limited use of verbal fillers	Pervasive use of multiple verbal fillers; uses one or two verbal fillers in most contributions; verbal fillers impede message
Fluency	Fluent speech	Stilted; hesitant; broken
Grammar and word choice	Uses proper grammar Uses correct word as correct part of speech; avoids use of slang or nonstandard English	Improper grammar usage Uses wrong word at times; uses correct word as wrong part of speech; pervasive use of slang or nonstandard English
Vocabulary	Extensive; demonstrates breadth of vocabulary	Limited
Volume, pitch, and tone	Volume and pitch are appropriate; tone is pleasant	Volume is too low or too high; pitch is unsettling to learners; tone is unpleasant or offensive

THINK AND WRITE

Compare the most recent peer assessment you received with previous peer assessments. Describe growth and remaining challenges with oral communication and the use of verbal fillers.

THINK AND WRITE

Explain how giving and receiving constructive feedback on performance is preparing you for giving and receiving constructive feedback as a classroom teacher.

📑 EXERCISE: "UMM GAME"—LEVEL THREE ("THIS I KNOW")

This stage should be the most challenging of all, so make certain that you have practiced sufficiently at Levels One and Two before proceeding.

Instructions: The instructor will bring a collection of quotes or guiding principles from the field of education. Many of those quotes or principles should have been previously discussed or found in assigned readings for the course. Each student will be given the quote or principle to be discussed, 10 seconds of "think time," and then he or she must accurately interpret the prompt—all the while avoiding using verbal fillers.

During this level, like Level Two, students may not use fictitious responses. Plausible statements of the meaning of the quote or guiding principle are to be shared.

Additionally, each student should have an assigned peer assessor who will complete the peer assessment form and also record the partner's impromptu speech for self-assessment purposes using a personal electronic device.

Examples:

> "It takes a village to raise a child."—African proverb
> Teachers lead by example.

[Script to be read by the Instructor]

"Class, we educators must be knowledgeable of the guiding principles and fundamental belief statements of our profession. Your classmate, [student's name], will be sharing [his or her] interpretation of [insert prompt here]. [Student Name], you may begin now...."

Over the course of the remaining 30 seconds, the speaker must address the assigned topic (as accurately as possible) while refraining from the use of "umm," "uhh," "like," repeated usages of "and," and other forms of verbal fillers. If at any point the speaker uses verbal fillers, the class *immediately* claps politely—encouraging the speaker to start over. The student speaker is asked to start over, and the clock is reset for 30 seconds.

The "Umm Game"—after repeated modeling—should be practiced in small groups and eventually expanded to impromptu speeches in front of the entire class.

LET'S TALK

As you listen to a classmate speak in the "This I Know" role of the "Umm Game"—Level THREE, complete the Peer Assessment 2.3 table. Upon completion of the peer assessment, use the sandwich language strategy (presented in Chapter 1) while sharing constructive feedback to your classmate in a positive manner.

Peer Assessment 2.6

Student's Name _____ Date _____

Behavior Indicators: Oral Communication

	ACCEPTABLE	**NEEDS IMPROVEMENT**
Use of verbal fillers	Free of verbal fillers; limited use of verbal fillers	Pervasive use of multiple verbal fillers; uses one or two verbal fillers in most contributions; verbal fillers impede message
Fluency	Fluent speech	Stilted; hesitant; broken
Grammar and word choice	Uses proper grammar Uses correct word as correct part of speech; avoids use of slang or nonstandard English	Improper grammar usage Uses wrong word at times; uses correct word as wrong part of speech; pervasive use of slang or nonstandard English
Vocabulary	Extensive; demonstrates breadth of vocabulary	Limited
Volume, pitch, and tone	Volume and pitch are appropriate; tone is pleasant	Volume is too low or too high; pitch is unsettling to learners; tone is unpleasant or offensive

🗐 EXERCISE

Take a minute to review the recording of your impromptu speech and self-assess using the following chart.

Self-Assessment 2.7

Student's Name _____ Date _____

Behavior Indicators: Oral Communication

	ACCEPTABLE	**NEEDS IMPROVEMENT**
Use of verbal fillers	Free of verbal fillers; limited use of verbal fillers	Pervasive use of multiple verbal fillers; uses one or two verbal fillers in most contributions; verbal fillers impede message
Fluency	Fluent speech	Stilted; hesitant; broken
Grammar and word choice	Uses proper grammar Uses correct word as correct part of speech; avoids use of slang or nonstandard English	Improper grammar usage Uses wrong word at times; uses correct word as wrong part of speech; pervasive use of slang or nonstandard English
Vocabulary	Extensive; demonstrates breadth of vocabulary	Limited
Volume, pitch, and tone	Volume and pitch are appropriate; tone is pleasant	Volume is too low or too high; pitch is unsettling to learners; tone is unpleasant or offensive

🖋 THINK AND WRITE

You have delivered numerous impromptu speeches to date. Overall, do you believe that your speech is creating a more favorable impression of your intellect, education, and competence than it did at the beginning of the course? Explain your answer.

📝 THINK AND WRITE

You have completed numerous impromptu speeches recently, each delivered with the intent of eliminating verbal fillers. Which verbal filler(s) are you most tempted to use now?

How often do you hear yourself using that and other fillers? (all of the time, most of the time, some of the time, and not very often)

Why do you think that is the case?

PRACTICE, PRACTICE, PRACTICE

So where do we go from here? Well, if you were an athlete who made only 40% of your free throws, your coach would help you diagnose the problem with your shot, show you how to correct the problem, and then tell you to practice, practice, practice. If you were a musician who struggled reading music, your teacher would prescribe the same.

For a teacher-in-training, the prescription is the same. Practice. Not half-hearted practice or "I'll do it when I feel like it" practice. The type of practice required to begin this new way of life (imagine trumpets sounding here) is 24 hours per day/7 days per week. Make a commitment to yourself and your future students that you will not go back to your old pattern of speech.

THINK AND WRITE

Forming new habits requires discipline, and discipline is predicated upon perseverance. Recall a time you broke an old habit and successfully replaced it with a new way of living. What strategies ensured your success in that situation? What strategies and commitments will you employ for this fresh start?

THINK AND WRITE

On a scale of 1–6 (6 = highest; 3 = average; 1 = poor), how would you rate your proficiency in oral communication? Explain how you arrived at that score.

EDUCATION TERMINOLOGY

2.2
CHAPTER

OBJECTIVES

The learner will:

- define key terms regularly used in the field of education and
- begin compiling a personal glossary of terms deemed "educational jargon."

It is not enough to simply remove verbal fillers from one's speech. It is also of great importance that one develops proficiency with the language of one's chosen profession. By developing basic proficiency in speaking and understanding the language of the field of education, you will become more conversant with professional educators who can mentor you into this noble profession.

VIGNETTE 2.2

> "TEAM has requested that you attended an IEP this afternoon to discuss Tom's progress in the PPI program. The PT and OT will also be present to discuss how effectively Tom's IEP. . . ."

Did you follow that? Likely not.

Professional educators have a language all of their own, so let us explore some of the most common terms you will encounter as you enter this noble profession.

Figure 2.8 Common Terms

Assessment
Collaboration with Stakeholders
Content knowledge/content area
Common Core
Content Expectations (state-specific)
Curriculum
Curriculum Framework
Dispositions
Diversity
Management and Organization
Pedagogy
Profession
Professional Disposition
Smarter Balanced Assessment
Standards/benchmarks
Title I

This list of common terms is by no means exhaustive. There are additional lists of terms commonly used in specializations within the field such as special education and elementary education. If you are seeking certification in either of those specializations, I would encourage you to develop a glossary for those field-specific terms as well.

WEBCONNECT

Search for .edu websites that provide field-specific definitions for the education terms listed below. Browse for additional terms that are commonly used in your area of specialization as well.

🎤 LET'S TALK

With a partner or in a small group, share your previous experiences learning a second language. What strategies seemed to work best for you? How can you employ similar strategies as you learn this new language: the language of professional educators?

📝 THINK AND WRITE

Reflect upon the experiences and strategies shared in the previous discussion. Which strategies would you like to use when learning the language of educators? Explain.

📑 EXERCISE: PERSONAL GLOSSARY

As you begin observing and volunteering in classrooms and other educational settings, you should become a "collector" of the terms of the profession. Be certain to record these terms on the following pages. For each term, be certain to follow the model provided:

Column One: Write out the word you heard or saw.

Column Two: Write out your best guess as to what the word means.

Column Three: Record the dictionary definition of the word.

Column Four: ask your instructor, field experience supervisor, classroom teacher, or other school personnel to explain what the term means, and then write down a condensed version of the explanation.

EXAMPLE:

WORD	"Best Guess" Definition	Dictionary Definition	Explanation Provided by an Educator
CURRICULUM	The lesson plans teachers use	"The courses offered by an educational institution" (Merriam-webster.com)	What is to be taught in every subject at every grade level

Figure 2.9

(See Appendix for additional glossary pages.)

Personal Glossary: Education Terms

WORD	"Best Guess" Definition	Dictionary Definition	Explanation Provided by an Educator
CURRICULUM	The lesson plans teachers use	"The courses offered by an educational institution" (Merriam-webster.com)	What is to be taught in every subject at every grade level

Personal Glossary: Education Terms

WORD	"Best Guess" Definition	Dictionary Definition	Explanation Provided by an Educator

Effective educators have a strong command of the language of their field. Although that is true, it is appropriate to share some related words of caution. These commonly used terms are deemed *jargon*—words that are field-specific and, therefore, difficult to understand by others outside of the profession. (Do you recall how you felt reading Vignette 2.2?)

Therefore, the reality is that—though you must master the jargon to effectively communicate with colleagues, administrators, and other school-related personnel—you must use these terms sparingly with other educational stakeholders such as students and their families. An example follows:

To a colleague, you may regularly use the terms *curriculum* and *Common Core* and *assessments.*

To a student's family, you should consider using phrasing such as "lessons that must be taught" and "testing."

📝 THINK AND WRITE

What are the most valuable insights you gleaned from Part I in this chapter? Share 3–5 insights in a bulleted list.

✍ THINK AND WRITE

What are the most valuable insights you gleaned from Part II in this chapter? Share 3–5 insights in a bulleted list.

INTERPERSONAL SKILLS

Numerous studies of hiring practices of K-12 schools indicated that "academic ability was considered subordinate to interpersonal skills."

Guarino, Santibanez, and Daley (2006, p. 184)

It is one thing to speak clearly and efficiently, but quite another to facilitate effective communication within a group. To that end, one must become a student of a complex dance comprising speaking and listening, observing and interpreting nonverbal messages, and responding appropriately to both. Teachers who demonstrate proficiency with interpersonal skills are able to build community within their classrooms and develop valuable partnerships with families and other educational stakeholders. As the aforementioned quote also suggests, teachers who demonstrate effective interpersonal skills are more likely to be hired as K-12 teachers. Many employers weigh a teacher's interpersonal skills even more heavily than their academic skills.

Therefore, this chapter affixes the spotlight on the development of interpersonal skills. While the focus of Chapter 1 was clarity of the spoken word and expansion of education-related vocabulary, this chapter attends to the many dimensions of nonverbal communication. Lesson One emphasizes acceptable physical mannerisms that contribute to teacher presence. Lesson Two spotlights behaviors that indicate active and empathic listening. Lesson Three offers guidance on the art and science of collaboration.

NONVERBAL COMMUNICATION

3.1
CHAPTER

The most important thing in communication is hearing what isn't said.

Peter F. Drucker

Effective teachers are often lauded for a single distinguishing attribute: *teacher presence*. Simply stated, teacher presence is the seemingly effortless manner by which a teacher engages learners and commands the attention of a group. Before most preservice teachers can perfect teacher presence, they must first self-assess and refine their verbal and nonverbal communication tendencies that influence teacher presence.

In this introductory lesson to nonverbal communication, we focus on the physical mannerisms that comprise nonverbal communication. Conventional wisdom suggests that the vast majority of communication—perhaps as much as 90% or more—is nonverbal. Such a significant proportion of a teacher's propensity for communication merits considerable attention and professional development.

OBJECTIVES

The learner will:

- develop self-awareness of physical mannerisms while standing and seated;
- self-assess proficiency in nonverbal communication;
- practice and refine effective nonverbal communication skills such as eye contact, facial expression, gestures, presence, and posture;
- reflect upon self-assessment and peer assessment of practice performances; and
- develop an understanding of the term *teacher presence* in context of the field of education.

Nonverbal communication is comprised of numerous components: physical mannerisms (including eye contact, facial expressions, and gestures), voice regulation, proxemics (how close one stands to another), and more. Throughout this lesson, you will practice your oral communication skills while paying close attention to your nonverbal communication tendencies. The feedback that you will give and receive throughout these exercises will be focused primarily on physical mannerisms.

Before beginning the practice exercises, read the "Behavior Indicators" table below and then complete the "Think and Write" prompts that immediately follow.

Table 3.1

Behavior Indicators: Physical Mannerisms while Standing

	ACCEPTABLE	NEEDS IMPROVEMENT
Hand placement	Hands resting comfortably at sides; hands clasped loosely below waist	Hands in pockets; wringing hands; hands on hips; hand twisting hair
Hand gestures	Periodic, meaningful gestures	Ongoing movements that lack meaning or appear distracting; fumbling with an object (clicking pen, twisting sleeve, jiggling change, etc.)
Distribution of weight	Weight distributed evenly across hips	Leaning (on to one hip, against an object)
Posture	Straight but not stiff; shoulders back	Slouching; stiff
Eye contact	Sustained; casually scanning across the audience	Evasive; staring in a single direction; fixed on the floor
Facial expression	Affect appropriate to setting or topic; relaxed lips or smile	Blunted or flat affect; pursed lips; biting lips; downward turn to mouth; furrowed brow
Presence	Confident; poised; commanding	Unsure; timid; indifferent; agitated; aggressive

THINK AND WRITE

As you review the list of acceptable mannerisms, which of the indicators did you find most surprising or helpful? Explain. Which of your mannerisms require the most improvement?

◈ THINK AND WRITE

Regarding mannerisms that require improvement, which of the indicators did you find most surprising or helpful? Which will be the most challenging for you to address? Explain.

▶ SHOW ME

Take a few minutes to view preservice teachers as they introduce themselves to a group. Attend closely to mannerisms, taking note of those which should be emulated.

As you complete the exercises that follow, remain conscious of your word choice and verbal fillers. However, place considerable effort into managing your physical mannerisms.

▤ EXERCISE: *TEACHER PRESENCE*—LEVEL ONE (STANDING)

[Script to be read by the Instructor to the class following a viewing of the "Teacher Presence" video clip]

"Learners, the following exercise provides each of you with the opportunity to practice appropriate nonverbal communication skills while responding to questions that our P-12 partners or hiring committees are likely to ask. In 'Umm Game' fashion, we will practice in small groups before we practice in front of the entire class.

Each speaker will be given up to 2 minutes to respond to the prompt provided. Before the first speaker begins, make certain that all speakers have a peer evaluator who completes the peer-evaluation form (Figure 3.3) during the exercise and makes a digital recording using the speaker's personal electronic device.

In addition, establish group norms for the silent signals that will be used to subtly alert speakers to the use of verbal crutches during their talks. However, make certain that the alerts do not cause the speaker to start completely over. Examples of silent signals could be a raised finger, a touch to the nose, and so forth.

For Exercises 3A, 3B, and 3C, be certain to use the same self-assessment and peer-assessment protocol. You may begin."

EXERCISE 3A SPEAKING PROMPT

"Please share a brief description of your teaching-related experiences. Examples may include, but are not limited to, camp counseling, babysitting, coaching, and mentoring. If time permits, explain how those experiences will benefit your teaching performance."

Now that you have completed the exercise, take a moment to self-assess using the table provided. After you have completed the self-assessment, ask a classmate to complete the peer-assessment form so that you may receive more feedback on your performance.

Table 3.2

Self-Assessment: Physical Mannerisms while Standing

Student's Name _____ Date _____

	ACCEPTABLE	NEEDS IMPROVEMENT
Hand placement	Hands resting comfortably at sides; hands clasped loosely below waist	Hands in pockets; wringing hands; hands on hips; hand twisting hair
Hand gestures	Periodic, meaningful gestures	Ongoing movements that lack meaning or appear distracting; fumbling with an object (clicking pen, twisting sleeve, jiggling change, etc.)
Distribution of weight	Weight distributed evenly across hips	Leaning (on to one hip, against an object)
Posture	Straight but not stiff; shoulders back	Slouching; stiff
Eye contact	Sustained; casually scanning across the audience	Evasive; staring in a single direction; fixed on the floor
Facial expression	Affect appropriate to setting or topic; relaxed lips or smile	Blunted or flat affect; pursed lips; biting lips; downward turn to mouth; furrowed brow
Presence	Confident; poised; commanding	Unsure; timid; indifferent; agitated; aggressive

LET'S TALK

As you observe your peer completing Exercise 3A, "Teaching-Related Experience," complete the peer assessment using the table provided. Upon completion of the peer assessment, use the sandwich language strategy (presented in Chapter 1) while sharing constructive feedback to your classmate in a positive manner.

Table 3.3

Peer-Assessment: Physical Mannerisms while Standing

Speaker's Name _____ Date _____

Peer Assessor's Name _____ Date _____

	ACCEPTABLE	NEEDS IMPROVEMENT
Hand placement	Hands resting comfortably at sides; hands clasped loosely below waist	Hands in pockets; wringing hands; hands on hips; hand twisting hair
Hand gestures	Periodic, meaningful gestures	Ongoing movements that lack meaning or appear distracting; fumbling with an object (clicking pen, twisting sleeve, jiggling change, etc.)
Distribution of weight	Weight distributed evenly across hips	Leaning (on to one hip, against an object)
Posture	Straight but not stiff; shoulders back	Slouching; stiff
Eye contact	Sustained; casually scanning across the audience	Evasive; staring in a single direction; fixed on the floor
Facial expression	Affect appropriate to setting or topic; relaxed lips or smile	Blunted or flat affect; pursed lips; biting lips; downward turn to mouth; furrowed brow
Presence	Confident; poised; commanding	Unsure; timid; indifferent; agitated; aggressive

THINK AND WRITE

Compare the two assessments you have before you: the peer assessment of your speaking and the self-assessment of your speaking. How accurate was your self-assessment? Explain. What are your strengths? In which area(s) must you target improvement?

PRACTICE, PRACTICE, PRACTICE

Before moving on to the next level, we will complete this same exercise using different prompts.

 EXERCISE 3B SPEAKING PROMPT

"Please share your passions in life."

Now that you have completed the exercise, take a moment to self-assess using the table provided. After you have completed the self-assessment, ask a classmate to complete the peer-assessment form so that you may receive more feedback on your performance.

Table 3.4

Self-Assessment: Physical Mannerisms while Standing

Student's Name _____ Date _____

	ACCEPTABLE	NEEDS IMPROVEMENT
Hand placement	Hands resting comfortably at sides; hands clasped loosely below waist	Hands in pockets; wringing hands; hands on hips; hand twisting hair
Hand gestures	Periodic, meaningful gestures	Ongoing movements that lack meaning or appear distracting; fumbling with an object (clicking pen, twisting sleeve, jiggling change, etc.)
Distribution of weight	Weight distributed evenly across hips	Leaning (on to one hip, against an object)
Posture	Straight but not stiff; shoulders back	Slouching; stiff
Eye contact	Sustained; casually scanning across the audience	Evasive; staring in a single direction; fixed on the floor
Facial expression	Affect appropriate to setting or topic; relaxed lips or smile	Blunted or flat affect; pursed lips; biting lips; downward turn to mouth; furrowed brow
Presence	Confident; poised; commanding	Unsure; timid; indifferent; agitated; aggressive

LET'S TALK

As you observe your peer completing Exercise 3B, "Passions," complete the peer-assessment using the table provided. Upon completion of the peer assessment, use the sandwich language strategy (presented in Chapter 1) while sharing constructive feedback with your classmate in a positive manner.

Table 3.5

Peer-Assessment: Physical Mannerisms while Standing

Speaker's Name _____ Date _____

Peer Assessor's Name _____ Date _____

	ACCEPTABLE	NEEDS IMPROVEMENT
Hand placement	Hands resting comfortably at sides; hands clasped loosely below waist	Hands in pockets; wringing hands; hands on hips; hand twisting hair
Hand gestures	Periodic, meaningful gestures	Ongoing movements that lack meaning or appear distracting; fumbling with an object (clicking pen, twisting sleeve, jiggling change, etc.)
Distribution of weight	Weight distributed evenly across hips	Leaning (on to one hip, against an object)
Posture	Straight but not stiff; shoulders back	Slouching; stiff
Eye contact	Sustained; casually scanning across the audience	Evasive; staring in a single direction; fixed on the floor
Facial expression	Affect appropriate to setting or topic; relaxed lips or smile	Blunted or flat affect; pursed lips; biting lips; downward turn to mouth; furrowed brow
Presence	Confident; poised; commanding	Unsure; timid; indifferent; agitated; aggressive

THINK AND WRITE

Compare the two assessments you have before you: the peer assessment of your speaking and the self-assessment of your speaking. How accurate was your self-assessment? Explain. What are your strengths? In which area(s) must you target improvement?

PRACTICE, PRACTICE, PRACTICE
EXERCISE 3C SPEAKING PROMPT

"Please share how your passions in life relate to teaching and/or can be incorporated into your teaching."

Now that you have completed the exercise, take a moment to self-assess using the table provided. After you have completed the self-assessment, ask a classmate to complete the peer-assessment form so that you may receive more feedback on your performance.

Table 3.6

Self-Assessment: Physical Mannerisms while Standing

Student's Name _____ Date _____

	ACCEPTABLE	NEEDS IMPROVEMENT
Hand placement	Hands resting comfortably at sides; hands clasped loosely below waist	Hands in pockets; wringing hands; hands on hips; hand twisting hair
Hand gestures	Periodic, meaningful gestures	Ongoing movements that lack meaning or appear distracting; fumbling with an object (clicking pen, twisting sleeve, jiggling change, etc.)
Distribution of weight	Weight distributed evenly across hips	Leaning (on to one hip, against an object)
Posture	Straight but not stiff; shoulders back	Slouching; stiff
Eye contact	Sustained; casually scanning across the audience	Evasive; staring in a single direction; fixed on the floor
Facial expression	Affect appropriate to setting or topic; relaxed lips or smile	Blunted or flat affect; pursed lips; biting lips; downward turn to mouth; furrowed brow
Presence	Confident; poised; commanding	Unsure; timid; indifferent; agitated; aggressive

 LET'S TALK

As you observe your peer completing Exercise 3C, "Passions," complete the peer-assessment using the table provided. Upon completion of the peer assessment, use the sandwich language strategy (presented in Chapter 1) while sharing constructive feedback with your classmate in a positive manner.

Table 3.7

Peer-Assessment: Physical Mannerisms while Standing

Speaker's Name _____ Date _____

Peer Assessor's Name _____ Date _____

	ACCEPTABLE	NEEDS IMPROVEMENT
Hand placement	Hands resting comfortably at sides; hands clasped loosely below waist	Hands in pockets; wringing hands; hands on hips; hand twisting hair
Hand gestures	Periodic, meaningful gestures	Ongoing movements that lack meaning or appear distracting; fumbling with an object (clicking pen, twisting sleeve, jiggling change, etc.)
Distribution of weight	Weight distributed evenly across hips	Leaning (on to one hip, against an object)
Posture	Straight but not stiff; shoulders back	Slouching; stiff
Eye contact	Sustained; casually scanning across the audience	Evasive; staring in a single direction; fixed on the floor
Facial expression	Affect appropriate to setting or topic; relaxed lips or smile	Blunted or flat affect; pursed lips; biting lips; downward turn to mouth; furrowed brow
Presence	Confident; poised; commanding	Unsure; timid; indifferent; agitated; aggressive

THINK AND WRITE

Compare the two assessments you have before you: the peer assessment of your speaking and the self-assessment of your speaking. How accurate was your self-assessment? Explain. What are your strengths? In which area(s) must you target improvement?

EXERCISE: *TEACHER PRESENCE*—LEVEL TWO (SEATED)

For Level Two of this exercise, we will repeat the same processes, but from a different position (literally). You will complete this process while seated. "Seated?!" you exclaim? "Why seated?" The answer is simple. As a professional educator, you will need to be an extremely effective communicator in numerous settings that require a seated position:

- Interviews
  - for admission into the teacher education program;
  - for a placement in a K-12 school for observation hours, field experiences, and student teaching; and
  - for a teaching position once you have been certified.
- Parent–teacher conferences.
- Parent meetings.
- Principal–teacher meetings to discuss your teacher evaluation and professional development.
- Staff meetings with colleagues.

Are you convinced that you will need to develop proficiency in this area? Then it is time to get started. Arrange the room in such a way that you are seated in a chair (preferably one with castors) facing your audience. The ideal room arrangement is to have a circle of chairs for small groups of students to complete this exercise.

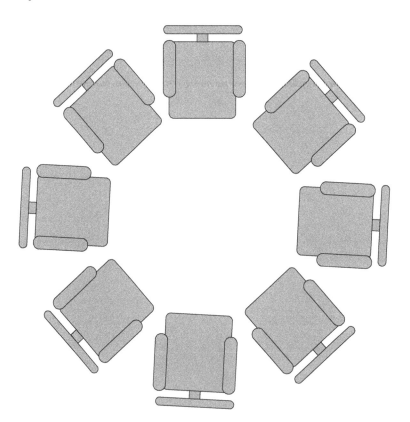

Following the protocol established during Level One, complete Level Two and the related assessments for each of the following prompts.

PRACTICE, PRACTICE, PRACTICE
EXERCISE 3D SPEAKING PROMPT

"Share your reasons for becoming a teacher. Consider making reference to your passions, previous affirming experiences, and your desires or calling."

Now that you have completed the exercise, take a moment to self-assess using the table provided. After you have completed the self-assessment, ask a classmate to complete the peer-assessment form so that you may receive more feedback on your performance.

Table 3.8

Self-Assessment: Physical Mannerisms while Seated

Student's Name _____ Date _____

	ACCEPTABLE	NEEDS IMPROVEMENT
Hand placement	Hands resting comfortably at sides; hands clasped loosely below waist	Hands in pockets; wringing hands; hands on hips; hand twisting hair
Hand gestures	Periodic, meaningful gestures	Ongoing movements that lack meaning or appear distracting; fumbling with an object (clicking pen, twisting sleeve, jiggling change, etc.)
Legs	Sit forward in seat so that knees are together, both feet are on the floor, and legs are not crossed	Legs swinging; chair swiveling side to side; legs wide apart; crossed legs that cause you to lean back in a chair; crossed legs that cause a skirt to go above the knee
Posture	Straight but not stiff; shoulders back	Slouching; stiff
Eye contact	Sustained; casually scanning across the audience	Evasive; staring in a single direction; fixed on the floor
Facial expression	Affect appropriate to setting or topic; relaxed lips or smile	Blunted or flat affect; pursed lips; biting lips; downward turn to mouth; furrowed brow
Presence	Confident; poised; commanding	Unsure; timid; indifferent; agitated; aggressive

LET'S TALK

As you observe your peer completing Exercise 3D "Reasons," complete the peer-assessment using the table provided. Upon completion of the peer assessment, use the sandwich language strategy (presented in Chapter 1) while sharing constructive feedback with your classmate in a positive manner.

Table 3.9

Peer-Assessment: Physical Mannerisms while Seated

Speaker's Name _____ Date _____

Peer Assessor's Name _____ Date _____

	ACCEPTABLE	NEEDS IMPROVEMENT
Hand placement	Hands resting comfortably at sides; hands clasped loosely below waist	Hands in pockets; wringing hands; hands on hips; hand twisting hair
Hand gestures	Periodic, meaningful gestures	Ongoing movements that lack meaning or appear distracting; fumbling with an object (clicking pen, twisting sleeve, jiggling change, etc.)
Legs	Sit forward in seat so that knees are together, both feet are on the floor, and legs are not crossed	Legs swinging; chair swiveling side to side; legs wide apart; crossed legs that cause you to lean back in a chair; crossed legs that cause a skirt to go above the knee
Posture	Straight but not stiff; shoulders back	Slouching; stiff
Eye contact	Sustained; casually scanning across the audience	Evasive; staring in a single direction; fixed on the floor
Facial expression	Affect appropriate to setting or topic; relaxed lips or smile	Blunted or flat affect; pursed lips; biting lips; downward turn to mouth; furrowed brow
Presence	Confident; poised; commanding	Unsure; timid; indifferent; agitated; aggressive

📝 **THINK AND WRITE**

Compare the two assessments. How accurate was your self-assessment? What are your strengths? In which area(s) must you target improvement?

🗐 **EXERCISE 3E   SPEAKING PROMPT**

"Share your preferences at this time for level of certification, your 'ideal' grade and/or subject area to teach, and any particular student populations you hope to serve. The populations you identify may include but are not limited to socioeconomic status, ethnicity, religion, or learning differences."

Now that you have completed the exercise, take a moment to self-assess using the table provided. After you have completed the self-assessment, ask a classmate to complete the peer-assessment form so that you may receive more feedback on your performance.

Table 3.10

Self-Assessment: Physical Mannerisms while Seated

Student's Name _____ Date _____

	ACCEPTABLE	NEEDS IMPROVEMENT
Hand placement	Hands resting comfortably at sides; hands clasped loosely below waist	Hands in pockets; wringing hands; hands on hips; hand twisting hair
Hand gestures	Periodic, meaningful gestures	Ongoing movements that lack meaning or appear distracting; fumbling with an object (clicking pen, twisting sleeve, jiggling change, etc.)
Legs	Sit forward in seat so that knees are together, both feet are on the floor, and legs are not crossed	Legs swinging; chair swiveling side to side; legs wide apart; crossed legs that cause you to lean back in a chair; crossed legs that cause a skirt to go above the knee
Posture	Straight but not stiff; shoulders back	Slouching; stiff
Eye contact	Sustained; casually scanning across the audience	Evasive; staring in a single direction; fixed on the floor
Facial expression	Affect appropriate to setting or topic; relaxed lips or smile	Blunted or flat affect; pursed lips; biting lips; downward turn to mouth; furrowed brow
Presence	Confident; poised; commanding	Unsure; timid; indifferent; agitated; aggressive

LET'S TALK

As you observe your peer completing Exercise 3E, "Certification," complete the peer-assessment using the table provided. Upon completion of the peer assessment, use the sandwich language strategy (presented in Chapter 1) while sharing constructive feedback with your classmate in a positive manner.

Table 3.11

Peer-Assessment: Physical Mannerisms while Seated

Speaker's Name _____ Date _____

Peer Assessor's Name _____ Date _____

	ACCEPTABLE	NEEDS IMPROVEMENT
Hand placement	Hands resting comfortably at sides; hands clasped loosely below waist	Hands in pockets; wringing hands; hands on hips; hand twisting hair
Hand gestures	Periodic, meaningful gestures	Ongoing movements that lack meaning or appear distracting; fumbling with an object (clicking pen, twisting sleeve, jiggling change, etc.)
Legs	Sit forward in seat so that knees are together, both feet are on the floor, and legs are not crossed	Legs swinging; chair swiveling side to side; legs wide apart; crossed legs that cause you to lean back in a chair; crossed legs that cause a skirt to go above the knee
Posture	Straight but not stiff; shoulders back	Slouching; stiff
Eye contact	Sustained; casually scanning across the audience	Evasive; staring in a single direction; fixed on the floor
Facial expression	Affect appropriate to setting or topic; relaxed lips or smile	Blunted or flat affect; pursed lips; biting lips; downward turn to mouth; furrowed brow
Presence	Confident; poised; commanding	Unsure; timid; indifferent; agitated; aggressive

📝 THINK AND WRITE

Compare the two assessments. How accurate was your self-assessment? What are your strengths? In which area(s) must you target improvement?

📑 EXERCISE 3F   SPEAKING PROMPT

"Share your preferences for the school setting which is most appealing to you at this time. Which of the following: urban, rural, or suburban settings, are you most inclined to pursue? Explain why."

Now that you have completed the exercise, take a moment to self-assess using the table provided. After you have completed the self-assessment, ask a classmate to complete the peer-assessment form so that you may receive more feedback on your performance.

Table 3.12

Self-Assessment: Physical Mannerisms while Seated

Student's Name _____ Date _____

	ACCEPTABLE	NEEDS IMPROVEMENT
Hand placement	Hands resting comfortably at sides; hands clasped loosely below waist	Hands in pockets; wringing hands; hands on hips; hand twisting hair
Hand gestures	Periodic, meaningful gestures	Ongoing movements that lack meaning or appear distracting; fumbling with an object (clicking pen, twisting sleeve, jiggling change, etc.)
Legs	Sit forward in seat so that knees are together, both feet are on the floor, and legs are not crossed	Legs swinging; chair swiveling side to side; legs wide apart; crossed legs that cause you to lean back in a chair; crossed legs that cause a skirt to go above the knee
Posture	Straight but not stiff; shoulders back	Slouching; stiff
Eye contact	Sustained; casually scanning across the audience	Evasive; staring in a single direction; fixed on the floor
Facial expression	Affect appropriate to setting or topic; relaxed lips or smile	Blunted or flat affect; pursed lips; biting lips; downward turn to mouth; furrowed brow
Presence	Confident; poised; commanding	Unsure; timid; indifferent; agitated; aggressive

LET'S TALK

As you observe your peer completing Exercise 3F "Settings," complete the peer-assessment using the table provided. Upon completion of the peer assessment, use the sandwich language strategy (presented in Chapter 1) while sharing constructive feedback to your classmate in a positive manner.

Table 3.13

Peer-Assessment: Physical Mannerisms while Seated

Speaker's Name _____ Date _____

Peer Assessor's Name _____ Date _____

	ACCEPTABLE	NEEDS IMPROVEMENT
Hand placement	Hands resting comfortably at sides; hands clasped loosely below waist	Hands in pockets; wringing hands; hands on hips; hand twisting hair
Hand gestures	Periodic, meaningful gestures	Ongoing movements that lack meaning or appear distracting; fumbling with an object (clicking pen, twisting sleeve, jiggling change, etc.)
Legs	Sit forward in seat so that knees are together, both feet are on the floor, and legs are not crossed	Legs swinging; chair swiveling side to side; legs wide apart; crossed legs that cause you to lean back in a chair; crossed legs that cause a skirt to go above the knee
Posture	Straight but not stiff; shoulders back	Slouching; stiff
Eye contact	Sustained; casually scanning across the audience	Evasive; staring in a single direction; fixed on the floor
Facial expression	Affect appropriate to setting or topic; relaxed lips or smile	Blunted or flat affect; pursed lips; biting lips; downward turn to mouth; furrowed brow
Presence	Confident; poised; commanding	Unsure; timid; indifferent; agitated; aggressive

📝 THINK AND WRITE

Compare the two assessments. How accurate was your self-assessment? What are your strengths? In which area(s) must you target improvement?

🗐 EXERCISE 3G   SPEAKING PROMPT

"Share your preferences for the type of school which most appeals to you at this time: public (traditional, charter, or magnet), private (religious or nonreligious), or international. Explain."

Now that you have completed the exercise, take a moment to self-assess using the table provided. After you have completed the self-assessment, ask a classmate to complete the peer-assessment form so that you may receive more feedback on your performance.

Table 3.14

Self-Assessment: Physical Mannerisms while Seated

Student's Name _____ Date _____

	ACCEPTABLE	NEEDS IMPROVEMENT
Hand placement	Hands resting comfortably at sides; hands clasped loosely below waist	Hands in pockets; wringing hands; hands on hips; hand twisting hair
Hand gestures	Periodic, meaningful gestures	Ongoing movements that lack meaning or appear distracting; fumbling with an object (clicking pen, twisting sleeve, jiggling change, etc.)
Legs	Sit forward in seat so that knees are together, both feet are on the floor, and legs are not crossed	Legs swinging; chair swiveling side to side; legs wide apart; crossed legs that cause you to lean back in a chair; crossed legs that cause a skirt to go above the knee
Posture	Straight but not stiff; shoulders back	Slouching; stiff
Eye contact	Sustained; casually scanning across the audience	Evasive; staring in a single direction; fixed on the floor
Facial expression	Affect appropriate to setting or topic; relaxed lips or smile	Blunted or flat affect; pursed lips; biting lips; downward turn to mouth; furrowed brow
Presence	Confident; poised; commanding	Unsure; timid; indifferent; agitated; aggressive

LET'S TALK

As you observe your peer completing Exercise 3F "Settings," complete the peer-assessment using the table provided. Upon completion of the peer assessment, use the sandwich language strategy (presented in Chapter 1) while sharing constructive feedback with your classmate in a positive manner.

Table 3.15

Peer-Assessment: Physical Mannerisms while Seated

Speaker's Name _____ Date _____

Peer Assessor's Name _____ Date _____

	ACCEPTABLE	NEEDS IMPROVEMENT
Hand placement	Hands resting comfortably at sides; hands clasped loosely below waist	Hands in pockets; wringing hands; hands on hips; hand twisting hair
Hand gestures	Periodic, meaningful gestures	Ongoing movements that lack meaning or appear distracting; fumbling with an object (clicking pen, twisting sleeve, jiggling change, etc.)
Legs	Sit forward in seat so that knees are together, both feet are on the floor, and legs are not crossed	Legs swinging; chair swiveling side to side; legs wide apart; crossed legs that cause you to lean back in a chair; crossed legs that cause a skirt to go above the knee
Posture	Straight but not stiff; shoulders back	Slouching; stiff
Eye contact	Sustained; casually scanning across the audience	Evasive; staring in a single direction; fixed on the floor
Facial expression	Affect appropriate to setting or topic; relaxed lips or smile	Blunted or flat affect; pursed lips; biting lips; downward turn to mouth; furrowed brow
Presence	Confident; poised; commanding	Unsure; timid; indifferent; agitated; aggressive

THINK AND WRITE

Compare the two assessments. How accurate was your self-assessment? What are your strengths? In which area(s) must you target improvement?

WEBCONNECT

Locate two or more websites that include descriptions of and techniques for developing teacher presence.

LET'S TALK

With a partner or in a small group, share what you have learned about teacher presence from your website review. In addition to the physical mannerisms you have practiced in this lesson, identify other mannerisms and techniques you will need to develop to ensure a strong teacher presence.

THINK AND WRITE

What is the relationship between clear speech and teacher presence? Include commonalities and differences in your analysis.

THINK AND WRITE

Compose a list of "Key Points to Remember" from this lesson.

ACTIVE LISTENING, EMPATHY, AND PERSONAL SPACE

There's a lot of difference between listening and hearing.

G.K. Chesterton

Chesterton's quote is more than merely a witty remark; it is an astute observation shared by teachers who understand that communication is both an art and a science. Effective teachers demonstrate adeptness in interpersonal communication by using active listening skills. Not only do they hear and attend to the spoken word, they also carefully attend to nonverbal cues as they seek to discern a speaker's intended message. In addition to actively listening, effective teachers demonstrate concern and understanding of a student's thoughts and feelings.

Active listening skills foster communication and facilitate the collaboration requisite for productive learning communities.Therefore, this section focuses on the development of active listening skills.

OBJECTIVES

The learner will:

- explain the differences between listening and hearing;
- develop an understanding of the terms active *listening, empathy,* and *personal space as* they are used in the field of education;
- develop self-awareness of nonverbal and verbal behaviors while working with others;
- practice and refine active listening skills, demonstrations of empathy, and appropriate use of personal space;
- self-assess proficiency in nonverbal communication; and
- reflect upon self-assessment and peer-assessment of practice performances.

HEARING VERSUS LISTENING

It is entirely possible for a person to hear every word spoken, yet not listen to an iota of the speaker's message. While hearing is limited to perceiving sound, listening is a more labor-intensive process composed of three distinct steps: receiving, attending, and assigning meaning (Tompkins, 2006). To receive a message, the listener gathers both auditory and visual stimuli. To attend to a message, the listener focuses upon the most pertinent stimuli while ignoring the rest. Finally, to assign meaning to the message, the listener must interpret the verbal and nonverbal communication sent.

THINK AND WRITE

In your own words, explain the differences between hearing and listening.

LET'S TALK

With a partner, share an example of an experience when you felt that someone heard you but did not listen. What mannerisms led you to conclude that the person was not listening? How did that make you feel? Explain.

THINK AND WRITE

Explain the relationship between effective teaching and active listening. How and to what extent does a teacher's ability to actively listen influence his or her relationship with students?

Though listening is preferable to hearing, *active* listening is the gold standard for effective educators. Students, families, and colleagues do not want simply to be heard—they want educators to listen. Active listening skills provide evidence that educators are truly paying attention to what is being said. Teachers who are prepared for the day ahead are able to truly actively listen to students as they enter the classroom versus those who are rushing around trying to prepare. Therefore, educators need to practice behaviors that demonstrate active listening skills.

Read the "Behavior Indicators" table below and then complete a self-assessment based upon your typical behaviors in school or other professional settings.

Table 3.16

Behavior Indicators: Active Listening Skills that Demonstrate Empathy

	ACCEPTABLE	NEEDS IMPROVEMENT
Eye contact	Conveys warmth and/or interest; sustained but not staring; casual "look aways" at least every 5 seconds	Conveys disinterest or lack of concern; staring; evasive
Facial expression	Affect appropriate to setting or topic; relaxed lips; smiling or frowning as it mirrors the speaker's message	Blunted or flat affect; pursed lips; nonresponsive to the spoken message
Body language	Occasional head nodding; body turned toward speaker	Body leaned back or turned away from speaker; crossed arms
Verbal affirmations	Occasional use of words and phrases such as "mmhmm," "yes," "okay," "I understand," and so forth	Silence; overuse of words and phrases that encourage the speaker to continue
Mirroring	Periodic interjections that summarize what has been spoken. Example: "If I understand you correctly, you are saying that . . ."	Interruptions; would-be listener commandeers the conversation or interjects unsolicited personal stories, advice, or judgments

THINK AND WRITE

Reflect upon your answers to the preceding self-assessment. Overall, do you believe your behaviors are at the "gold standard" for active listening skills of educators? Explain your answer.

LET'S TALK

In small groups, read each of the following quotes aloud and create consensus around what you believe the speaker is trying to say:

"You're short on ears and long on mouth."—John Wayne

"No one cares how much you know, until they know how much you care."—Theodore Roosevelt

"Self-absorption in all its forms kills empathy"—Daniel Goleman

"Most people do not listen with the intent to understand; they listen with the intent to reply."—Stephen R. Covey

📝 THINK AND WRITE

Record your favorite quote from those listed above. Explain why you have selected it as a favorite and how recalling this quote will help you succeed as a classroom teacher.

🌐 WEBCONNECT

Search the Internet to locate an "active listening" skill-building exercise that you can teach to a small group of your peers during the next class.

📝 THINK AND WRITE

Reduce the directions for the listening exercise you found into five bullet points or less. Record those points here, noting any visual demonstrations you will use when explaining the exercise to your peers.

LET'S TALK

In small groups, teach one another the skill-building exercises that you located through your web search. Discuss which of those exercises you would like to incorporate into your own classrooms in the future.

PERSONAL SPACE VERSUS INTIMATE SPACE

Have you ever heard someone express frustration, discomfort, or even anger because someone was in his or her "space"? When interacting with others in a standing or seated position, our use of space sends a message to others about our power, influence, and intentions.

Personal space is an important consideration for educators who collaborate with students, colleagues, and families on a daily basis. Though the "comfortable" distance between individuals varies from culture to culture, the acceptable distance for personal space in the United States is typically two and a half to four feet (Morse, 2008).

Consider for a moment the various interactions with other educational stakeholders that require an educator to approach another person's personal space:

- Parent–teacher conferences.
- Staff meetings.
- Casual interactions with caregivers in the hallway or on field trips.

An educator's use of space matters.

Think, for a moment, about general seating (coach) on an airplane. I dare say most people would describe these close quarters with others as somewhat uncomfortable. Why? Close proximity with strangers—often within the distance American culture would deem *intimate*—can be distressing. This encroachment of space goes beyond our *personal space* boundaries and heads into boundaries established for *intimate space*.

In contrast to personal space, *intimate space* is only 6–18 inches (Morse, 2008). In teaching settings, it is important that we do not violate others' intimate space. Whether it is an unwelcome touch on the shoulder or a pat on a head, educators need to be very conscious of the personal space boundaries established by the culture, the school district, and the individual involved.

THINK AND WRITE

Recall the boundaries established for personal space during your K-12 experience. What standards or policies were set in place for teacher to student contact? Were there different standards in the classroom as opposed to extracurricular settings (sports, music, drama, etc.)? Explain your feelings related to those standards and policies.

LET'S TALK

Recall experiences with K-12 educators, coaches, advisors, or support staff that may have encroached upon intimate space. Describe your feelings to a partner.

✍ THINK AND WRITE

After describing your "encroachment" stories, reflect upon the commonalities and differences among the stories you and your partner shared. When, if ever, is it acceptable for a professional educator to enter a student's intimate space? Explain.

🔎 WEBCONNECT

Review the "Personal Space and Touching" resource located at culturecrossing.net. Analyze the differences in various standards of personal space that exist from one country to another.

📝 THINK AND WRITE

Effective educators recognize that students and families may have different standards for personal space because of ethnic and cultural differences. Explain your plan for engaging and collaborating with diverse families in a professional manner that considers differing standards of personal space.

📝 THINK AND WRITE

What did you find most interesting in this section on the subject of hearing, listening, and active listening?

THINK AND WRITE

Compose a list of "Key Points to Remember" from this exploration of personal space versus intimate space.

COLLABORATION

Coming together is a beginning. Keeping together is progress. Working together is success.

Henry Ford

Effective teachers demonstrate proficiency in *collaboration*. They can play the role of either the leader or equal member of a group, and they know when it is appropriate to do so to accomplish goals of the group. Effective teachers share responsibility for group work and find ways to make positive contributions to the emotional climate and collaborative work at hand.

OBJECTIVES

The learner will:

- develop an understanding of the term *collaboration* as it is used in the field of education;
- develop self-awareness of personal behaviors while in collaborative group settings;
- self-assess proficiency in human interaction skills;
- practice and refine collaboration skills in an educational context such as active listening, rapport-building, perceptiveness, sensitivity, and posture; and
- reflect upon self-assessment and peer assessment of practice performances.

Effective collaboration is the product of individuals who are intentional in the way that they speak, listen, and respond to one another during the give-and-take exchange of ideas. Throughout this section of Chapter 3, you will practice your collaborations skills while paying close attention to your nonverbal communication tendencies. As in previous chapters, you will give and receive feedback throughout these exercises.

Before beginning the practice exercises, read the "Behavior Indicators" table below and then complete the "Think and Write" prompts that immediately follow.

Table 3.17

Behavior Indicators: Collaboration

	ACCEPTABLE	NEEDS IMPROVEMENT
Active listening skills	Occasional head nodding, appropriate eye contact, body turned toward speaker	No acknowledgment of speaker, inappropriate eye contact, body turned away from speaker
Rapport	Conveys warmth, positivity; facilitates connectedness or actively engages with others in the group	Appears distant, indifferent, or aloof; makes little or no effort to engage with others or respond to others' efforts to draw in
Perceptiveness, with-it-ness	Accurately reads verbal and nonverbal cues; recognizes needs of individuals and group	Does not respond appropriately to others' verbal and nonverbal cues; appears unaware of needs of individuals and group
Tolerant, sensitive	Supportive even if not in agreement; sensitive to others' feelings	Critical, judgmental, eye rolling; insensitive to others' feelings
Posture	Leans forward at times to demonstrate engagement; "open" body language	Leans back or away from group members; "closed" body language (arm folding, etc.)

📝 **THINK AND WRITE**

As you review the list of acceptable mannerisms, which of the indicators did you find most surprising or helpful? Explain. Which of your mannerisms will require the most improvement?

📝 **THINK AND WRITE**

Regarding mannerisms that will require improvement, which of the indicators did you find most surprising or helpful? Which will be the most challenging for you to address? Explain.

🌐 WEBCONNECT

A classic cooperative learning strategy that requires effective collaboration and full engagement of all participants is "Numbered Heads Together." Search the Internet for at least two websites that describe the Numbered Heads Together strategy. Prepare to use that strategy as you complete the exercises that follow.

▶ SHOW ME

Take a few minutes to view preservice teachers as they collaborate using the Number Heads Together strategy in a small group. Attend closely to mannerisms, taking note of those that should be emulated.

📑 EXERCISES: *COLLABORATION*

Before you complete each of the following exercises, determine which of the following means of assessment you will use for each activity.

Peer-Assessment Options

1. Groups take turns:

   With this option, each small group of students collaborates in a "fish bowl" sort of approach. The group that collaborates is in the center of the room. Classmates observe from the outside of the circle and complete the peer-assessment form for their assigned partner.

2. Designated videographers:

   Depending upon class size, a different group of students is deemed "videographer crew" for each exercise. Each of those students is assigned to digitally record one small group's collaborative session. For example, in a class size of 15, the instructor could establish three groups of four students. Each of the remaining students would be assigned one group to digitally record the collaborative exercise. The videographer role would change for every exercise.

Collaboration Discussion Prompts

[Script to be read by the Instructor to the class following a viewing of the "Collaboration" video clip and determination of peer-assessment means for each exercise. Before collaboration begins, make certain that all participants either have a peer evaluator who completes the peer-evaluation form during the exercise or that a designated videographer outside of the group makes a digital recording.]

"Learners, the following prompts are designed to generate lively discussions with differing opinions. Your task is to listen to one another's positions, and then arrive at a group consensus response. Be certain to practice appropriate collaboration skills while responding to these questions.

Each small group will be given up to 20 minutes to reach consensus on the prompt provided.

For all exercises, be certain to complete self-assessments after you review the digital recording.

As you complete the exercises that follow, remain conscious of your word choice and verbal fillers. However, place considerable effort into managing your behaviors that demonstrate engagement and best practice collaboration.

You may begin."

EXERCISE 3J   SPEAKING PROMPT

"What are the greatest advantages and disadvantages of teaching at the elementary grade level? Reach consensus on at least three for each."

Table 3.18

Behavior Indicators: Collaboration, Self-Assessment

	ACCEPTABLE	NEEDS IMPROVEMENT
Active listening skills	Occasional head nodding, appropriate eye contact, body turned toward speaker	No acknowledgment of speaker, inappropriate eye contact, body turned away from speaker
Rapport	Conveys warmth, positivity; facilitates connectedness or actively engages with others in the group	Appears distant, indifferent, or aloof; makes little or no effort to engage with others or respond to others' efforts to draw in
Perceptiveness, with-it-ness	Accurately reads verbal and non-verbal cues; recognizes needs of individuals and group	Does not respond appropriately to others' verbal and nonverbal cues; appears unaware of needs of individuals and group
Tolerant, sensitive	Supportive even if not in agreement; sensitive to others' feelings	Critical, judgmental, eye rolling; insensitive to others' feelings
Posture	Leans forward at times to demonstrate engagement; "open" body language	Leans back or away from group members; "closed" body language (arm folding, etc.)

Table 3.19

Behavior Indicators: Collaboration, Peer Assessment

	ACCEPTABLE	NEEDS IMPROVEMENT
Active listening skills	Occasional head nodding, appropriate eye contact, body turned toward speaker	No acknowledgment of speaker, inappropriate eye contact, body turned away from speaker
Rapport	Conveys warmth, positivity; facilitates connectedness or actively engages with others in the group	Appears distant, indifferent, or aloof; makes little or no effort to engage with others or respond to others' efforts to draw in
Perceptiveness, with-it-ness	Accurately reads verbal and non-verbal cues; recognizes needs of individuals and group	Does not respond appropriately to others' verbal and nonverbal cues; appears unaware of needs of individuals and group
Tolerant, sensitive	Supportive even if not in agreement; sensitive to others' feelings	Critical, judgmental, eye rolling; insensitive to others' feelings
Posture	Leans forward at times to demonstrate engagement; "open" body language	Leans back or away from group members; "closed" body language (arm folding, etc.)

LET'S TALK

Share key points of the peer assessment with the classmate whom you observed. Be certain to use the sandwich language strategy while sharing constructive feedback to your classmate in a positive manner.

EXERCISE 3K   SPEAKING PROMPT

"What are the greatest advantages and disadvantages of teaching at the secondary level? Reach consensus on at least three for each."

Table 3.20

Behavior Indicators: Collaboration, Self-Assessment

	ACCEPTABLE	NEEDS IMPROVEMENT
Active listening skills	Occasional head nodding, appropriate eye contact, body turned toward speaker	No acknowledgment of speaker, inappropriate eye contact, body turned away from speaker
Rapport	Conveys warmth, positivity; facilitates connectedness or actively engages with others in the group	Appears distant, indifferent, or aloof; makes little or no effort to engage with others or respond to others' efforts to draw in
Perceptiveness, with-it-ness	Accurately reads verbal and nonverbal cues; recognizes needs of individuals and group	Does not respond appropriately to others' verbal and nonverbal cues; appears unaware of needs of individuals and group
Tolerant, sensitive	Supportive even if not in agreement; sensitive to others' feelings	Critical, judgmental, eye rolling; insensitive to others' feelings
Posture	Leans forward at times to demonstrate engagement; "open" body language	Leans back or away from group members; "closed" body language (arm folding, etc.)

Table 3.21

Behavior Indicators: Collaboration, Peer Assessment

	ACCEPTABLE	NEEDS IMPROVEMENT
Active listening skills	Occasional head nodding, appropriate eye contact, body turned toward speaker	No acknowledgment of speaker, inappropriate eye contact, body turned away from speaker
Rapport	Conveys warmth, positivity; facilitates connectedness or actively engages with others in the group	Appears distant, indifferent, or aloof; makes little or no effort to engage with others or respond to others' efforts to draw in
Perceptiveness, with-it-ness	Accurately reads verbal and nonverbal cues; recognizes needs of individuals and group	Does not respond appropriately to others' verbal and nonverbal cues; appears unaware of needs of individuals and group
Tolerant, sensitive	Supportive even if not in agreement; sensitive to others' feelings	Critical, judgmental, eye rolling; insensitive to others' feelings
Posture	Leans forward at times to demonstrate engagement; "open" body language	Leans back or away from group members; "closed" body language (arm folding, etc.)

THINK AND WRITE

Compare the two assessments. How accurate was your self-assessment? What are your strengths? In which area(s) must you target improvement?

🗐 EXERCISE 3L   SPEAKING PROMPT

"What are the greatest advantages and disadvantages of teaching? Reach consensus on at least three for each."

Table 3.22

Behavior Indicators: Collaboration, Self-Assessment

	ACCEPTABLE	NEEDS IMPROVEMENT
Active listening skills	Occasional head nodding, appropriate eye contact, body turned toward speaker	No acknowledgment of speaker, inappropriate eye contact, body turned away from speaker
Rapport	Conveys warmth, positivity; facilitates connectedness or actively engages with others in the group	Appears distant, indifferent, or aloof; makes little or no effort to engage with others or respond to others' efforts to draw in
Perceptiveness, with-it-ness	Accurately reads verbal and nonverbal cues; recognizes needs of individuals and group	Does not respond appropriately to others' verbal and nonverbal cues; appears unaware of needs of individuals and group
Tolerant, sensitive	Supportive even if not in agreement; sensitive to others' feelings	Critical, judgmental, eye rolling; insensitive to others' feelings
Posture	Leans forward at times to demonstrate engagement; "open" body language	Leans back or away from group members; "closed" body language (arm folding, etc.)

Table 3.23

Behavior Indicators: Collaboration, Peer Assessment

	ACCEPTABLE	NEEDS IMPROVEMENT
Active listening skills	Occasional head nodding, appropriate eye contact, body turned toward speaker	No acknowledgment of speaker, inappropriate eye contact, body turned away from speaker
Rapport	Conveys warmth, positivity; facilitates connectedness or actively engages with others in the group	Appears distant, indifferent, or aloof; makes little or no effort to engage with others or respond to others' efforts to draw in
Perceptiveness, with-it-ness	Accurately reads verbal and nonverbal cues; recognizes needs of individuals and group	Does not respond appropriately to others' verbal and nonverbal cues; appears unaware of needs of individuals and group
Tolerant, sensitive	Supportive even if not in agreement; sensitive to others' feelings	Critical, judgmental, eye rolling; insensitive to others' feelings
Posture	Leans forward at times to demonstrate engagement; "open" body language	Leans back or away from group members; "closed" body language (arm folding, etc.)

LET'S TALK

Share key points of the peer assessment with the classmate whom you observed. Be certain to use the sandwich language strategy while sharing constructive feedback to your classmate in a positive manner.

EXERCISE 3M   SPEAKING PROMPT

"Which is the most difficult level to teach? (Elementary? Middle? High School?) Provide three reasons to support your answer. You must reach consensus."

Table 3.24

Behavior Indicators: Collaboration, Self-Assessment

	ACCEPTABLE	NEEDS IMPROVEMENT
Active listening skills	Occasional head nodding, appropriate eye contact, body turned toward speaker	No acknowledgment of speaker, inappropriate eye contact, body turned away from speaker
Rapport	Conveys warmth, positivity; facilitates connectedness or actively engages with others in the group	Appears distant, indifferent, or aloof; makes little or no effort to engage with others or respond to others' efforts to draw in
Perceptiveness, with-it-ness	Accurately reads verbal and nonverbal cues; recognizes needs of individuals and group	Does not respond appropriately to others' verbal and nonverbal cues; appears unaware of needs of individuals and group
Tolerant, sensitive	Supportive even if not in agreement; sensitive to others' feelings	Critical, judgmental, eye rolling; insensitive to others' feelings
Posture	Leans forward at times to demonstrate engagement; "open" body language	Leans back or away from group members; "closed" body language (arm folding, etc.)

Table 3.25

Behavior Indicators: Collaboration, Peer Assessment

	ACCEPTABLE	NEEDS IMPROVEMENT
Active listening skills	Occasional head nodding, appropriate eye contact, body turned toward speaker	No acknowledgment of speaker, inappropriate eye contact, body turned away from speaker
Rapport	Conveys warmth, positivity; facilitates connectedness or actively engages with others in the group	Appears distant, indifferent, or aloof; makes little or no effort to engage with others or respond to others' efforts to draw in
Perceptiveness, with-it-ness	Accurately reads verbal and non-verbal cues; recognizes needs of individuals and group	Does not respond appropriately to others' verbal and nonverbal cues; appears unaware of needs of individuals and group
Tolerant, sensitive	Supportive even if not in agreement; sensitive to others' feelings	Critical, judgmental, eye rolling; insensitive to others' feelings
Posture	Leans forward at times to demonstrate engagement; "open" body language	Leans back or away from group members; "closed" body language (arm folding, etc.)

THINK AND WRITE

Compare the two assessments. How accurate was your self-assessment? What are your strengths? In which area(s) must you target improvement?

EXERCISE 3N   SPEAKING PROMPT

"Imagine that you have been hired to revise the curriculum for this education course. You've been told that you must remove two homework assignments and one in-class exercise. What will you remove? Provide at least two solid reasons for each removal. You must reach consensus for the items you choose."

Table 3.26

Behavior Indicators: Collaboration, Self-Assessment

	ACCEPTABLE	NEEDS IMPROVEMENT
Active listening skills	Occasional head nodding, appropriate eye contact, body turned toward speaker	No acknowledgment of speaker, inappropriate eye contact, body turned away from speaker
Rapport	Conveys warmth, positivity; facilitates connectedness or actively engages with others in the group	Appears distant, indifferent, or aloof; makes little or no effort to engage with others or respond to others' efforts to draw in
Perceptiveness, with-it-ness	Accurately reads verbal and nonverbal cues; recognizes needs of individuals and group	Does not respond appropriately to others' verbal and nonverbal cues; appears unaware of needs of individuals and group
Tolerant, sensitive	Supportive even if not in agreement; sensitive to others' feelings	Critical, judgmental, eye rolling; insensitive to others' feelings
Posture	Leans forward at times to demonstrate engagement; "open" body language	Leans back or away from group members; "closed" body language (arm folding, etc.)

Table 3.27

Behavior Indicators: Collaboration, Peer Assessment

	ACCEPTABLE	NEEDS IMPROVEMENT
Active listening skills	Occasional head nodding, appropriate eye contact, body turned toward speaker	No acknowledgment of speaker, inappropriate eye contact, body turned away from speaker
Rapport	Conveys warmth, positivity; facilitates connectedness or actively engages with others in the group	Appears distant, indifferent, or aloof; makes little or no effort to engage with others or respond to others' efforts to draw in
Perceptiveness, with-it-ness	Accurately reads verbal and nonverbal cues; recognizes needs of individuals and group	Does not respond appropriately to others' verbal and nonverbal cues; appears unaware of needs of individuals and group
Tolerant, sensitive	Supportive even if not in agreement; sensitive to others' feelings	Critical, judgmental, eye rolling; insensitive to others' feelings
Posture	Leans forward at times to demonstrate engagement; "open" body language	Leans back or away from group members; "closed" body language (arm folding, etc.)

LET'S TALK

Share key points of the peer assessment with the classmate whom you observed. Be certain to use the sandwich language strategy while sharing constructive feedback to your classmate in a positive manner.

THINK AND WRITE

Compose a list of "Key Points to Remember" from these collaboration experiences.

WEBCONNECT

Search the Internet to locate another collaboration activity that you would like to use in your own classroom eventually.

LET'S TALK

Describe to a classmate the collaboration activity that you found.

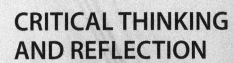

CRITICAL THINKING AND REFLECTION

4

If you can't explain it simply, you don't understand it well enough.

Albert Einstein

Complex thinking includes at least four distinct processes: problem solving, decision making, critical thinking, and creative thinking (Presseisen, 2001). Though numerous definitions circulate for *critical thinking*, a widely accepted definition of critical thinking is "the art of analyzing and evaluating thinking with a view to improving it" (Paul & Elder, 2008, p. 2). Reflective thinking is a specific part of the critical thinking process focused upon analyzing and making judgments of what has happened (Hawaii.edu).

Considering the centrality of critical thinking to a teacher's daily problem-solving and decision-making responsibilities, an entire lesson focused on professional development in this area is of tremendous merit. This entire workbook—not solely this chapter—is designed in such a way so as to foster critical thinking skills and, more specifically, the reflective thinking skills that effective teachers must employ daily to thrive.

OBJECTIVES

The learner will:

- refine critical thinking skills by focusing upon clarity, organization, logic, focus, and essential questions and
- employ critical thinking skills when solving problems deemed ethical or moral dilemmas.

Before we embark upon discussions of critical thinking, we must first look to elements of critical thinking and behavior indicators that reveal it.

LET'S TALK

In small groups, read and review the chart below. Brainstorm and discuss examples for each category listed.

Behavior Indicators: Critical Thinking

	ACCEPTABLE	NEEDS IMPROVEMENT
Clarity/organization	Clear, easy to follow, organized	Disorganized, muddled, confused
Logic	Analytical, thorough	Commits logical fallacies: • overgeneralization • misses the point • false cause • ad hominem • other
Level of abstraction	Firm grasp of conceptual Identifies principles at play in concrete experiences	Fixated on personal experience Does not make the connection between concrete experiences and underlying principles/theoretical
Focus	Focused on essentials • definition of problem • assumptions • evidence	Sidetracked on irrelevant information, impertinent details Not inclined to search for essentials or sort information for relevance
Questions	Poses relevant questions based upon essentials: • clarifications • assumptions • evidence • alternative perspectives	Does not question Asks nonessential questions

ESSENTIAL QUESTIONS

Effective teachers are competent thinkers who know how to ask the right sort of questions. James Collins, author of the best seller *Good to Great*, described the most effective leaders as hedgehogs: "Hedgehogs have a piercing insight that allows them to see through complexity and discern underlying patterns. Hedgehogs see what is essential, and ignore the rest."

Effective teacher leaders strive to be hedgehogs in this sense. One type of questioning, dating back to the time of Socrates, is called Socratic questioning. Focused upon questions of clarification, assumptions, reasoning, evidence, and alternative perspectives, these questions guide an individual to focus on esssentials.

⟨⟩ WEBCONNECT

The Internet is rich with credible websites that explain logical thinking. Using only .edu websites, OWL Purdue, or critical thinking.org, locate the following fundamental concepts:

- Using logic.
- Reaching logical conclusions.
- Socratic questions.

▤ EXERCISE: PAMPHLET

Compose a simple trifold pamphlet that explains the essentials of the aforementioned topics at a developmental level your students may understand. Additionally, include paraphrasing of excerpts of the chart that follows. If you are seeking licensure at the early childhood level, you may write for an upper elementary audience.

Guidelines for *Critical Thinking* Behaviors in Discussions of Moral Dilemmas

Now that we have established the absolute necessity that teacher leaders are critical thinkers, let us review those behaviors that constitute sound critical thinking.

Behavior Indicators of Critical Thinking Skills

	ACCEPTABLE	NEEDS IMPROVEMENT
Clarity/organization	Clear, easy to follow, organized	Disorganized, muddled, confused
Logic	Analytical, thorough	Commits logical fallacies: • overgeneralization • misses the point • false cause • ad hominem • other
Level of abstraction	Firm grasp of conceptual Identifies principles at play in concrete experiences	Fixated on personal experience Does not make the connection between concrete experiences and underlying principles/theoretical
Focus	Focused on essentials • definition of problem • assumptions • evidence	Sidetracked on irrelevant information, impertinent details Not inclined to search for essentials or sort information for relevance
Questions	Poses relevant questions based upon essentials: • clarifications • assumptions • evidence • alternative perspectives	Does not question Asks nonessential questions

LET'S TALK

In small groups, review the behavior indicators one last time. Seek out clarification from class-mates and the course instructor before continuing on to the next exercise. You will soon apply these skills as you solve moral dilemmas in small groups.

WEBCONNECT

Search the Internet using the phrases "moral dilemma," "classic moral dilemmas," and "ethical dilemmas." One excellent source is a document entitled "Numerous Dilemmas that Teachers Face" (http://www.ctteam.org/df/resources/Module5_Manual.pdf). Select the moral dilemmas that you as a class would like to examine using your newly developed critical thinking skills.

ASSESSMENT PREPARATION

Before you complete each of the following exercises, determine which of the following means of peer assessment you will use for each activity. The "Behavior Indicators: Leadership Skills" form will be used for both peer assessment and self-assessment.

Peer Assessment Options

1. Groups Take Turns
   With this option, each small group of students collaborates in a "fish bowl" sort of approach. The group that collaborates is in the center of the room. Classmates observe from the outside of the circle and complete the peer assessment form for their assigned partner.

2. Designated Videographers
   Depending upon class size, a different group of students is deemed "videographer crew" for each exercise. Each of those students is assigned to digitally record one small group's collaborative session. For example, in a class size of 15, the instructor could establish three groups of four students. Each of the remaining students would be assigned one group to digitally record the collaborative exercise. The videographer role would change for every exercise.

   Now is the time for you to begin practicing your critical thinking skills as you strive for consensus on the following ethical dilemmas.

📑 EXERCISE: MORAL DILEMMA #1

Self-Assessment: Behavior Indicators: Critical Thinking Skills
(if a digital recording was made)

Speaker's Name _____ Date _____

	ACCEPTABLE	NEEDS IMPROVEMENT
Clarity/organization	Clear, easy to follow, organized	Disorganized, muddled, confused
Logic	Analytical, thorough	Commits logical fallacies: • overgeneralization • misses the point • false cause • ad hominem • other
Level of abstraction	Firm grasp of conceptual Identifies principles at play in concrete experiences	Fixated on personal experience Does not make the connection between concrete experiences and underlying principles/theoretical
Focus	Focused on essentials • definition of problem • assumptions • evidence	Sidetracked on irrelevant information, impertinent details Not inclined to search for essentials or sort information for relevance
Questions	Poses relevant questions based upon essentials: • clarifications • assumptions • evidence • alternative perspectives	Does not question Asks nonessential questions

Peer-Assessment: Behavior Indicators: Critical Thinking Skills

Speaker's Name _____ Date _____

Peer Assessor's Name _____ Date _____

	ACCEPTABLE	NEEDS IMPROVEMENT
Clarity/organization	Clear, easy to follow, organized	Disorganized, muddled, confused
Logic	Analytical, thorough	Commits logical fallacies: • overgeneralization • misses the point • false cause • ad hominem • other
Level of abstraction	Firm grasp of conceptual Identifies principles at play in concrete experiences	Fixated on personal experience Does not make the connection between concrete experiences and underlying principles/theoretical
Focus	Focused on essentials • definition of problem • assumptions • evidence	Sidetracked on irrelevant information, impertinent details Not inclined to search for essentials or sort information for relevance
Questions	Poses relevant questions based upon essentials: • clarifications • assumptions • evidence • alternative perspectives	Does not question Asks nonessential questions

⟦≡⟧ EXERCISE: MORAL DILEMMA #2

Self-Assessment: Behavior Indicators: Critical Thinking Skills
(if a digital recording was made)

Speaker's Name _____ Date _____

	ACCEPTABLE	NEEDS IMPROVEMENT
Clarity/organization	Clear, easy to follow, organized	Disorganized, muddled, confused
Logic	Analytical, thorough	Commits logical fallacies: • overgeneralization • misses the point • false cause • ad hominem • other
Level of abstraction	Firm grasp of conceptual Identifies principles at play in concrete experiences	Fixated on personal experience Does not make the connection between concrete experiences and underlying principles/theoretical
Focus	Focused on essentials • definition of problem • assumptions • evidence	Sidetracked on irrelevant information, impertinent details Not inclined to search for essentials or sort information for relevance
Questions	Poses relevant questions based upon essentials: • clarifications • assumptions • evidence • alternative perspectives	Does not question Asks nonessential questions

Peer-Assessment: Behavior Indicators: Critical Thinking Skills

Speaker's Name _____ Date _____

Peer Assessor's Name _____ Date _____

	ACCEPTABLE	NEEDS IMPROVEMENT
Clarity/organization	Clear, easy to follow, organized	Disorganized, muddled, confused
Logic	Analytical, thorough	Commits logical fallacies: • overgeneralization • misses the point • false cause • ad hominem • other
Level of abstraction	Firm grasp of conceptual Identifies principles at play in concrete experiences	Fixated on personal experience Does not make the connection between concrete experiences and underlying principles/theoretical
Focus	Focused on essentials • definition of problem • assumptions • evidence	Sidetracked on irrelevant information, impertinent details Not inclined to search for essentials or sort information for relevance
Questions	Poses relevant questions based upon essentials: • clarifications • assumptions • evidence • alternative perspectives	Does not question Asks nonessential questions

▤ THINK AND WRITE

Compare the peer assessment feedback you received with your self-assessments. In which areas do you demonstrate the greatest competency? In which areas must you continue to strive and grow?

▤ THINK AND WRITE

What have you learned about logic and structures of logic as a result of the previous exercises? What do you still need to research or practice further?

THINK AND WRITE

Which features and exercises in this text foster critical thinking skills? Which features foster reflective thinking skills?

CRITICAL THINKING AND LOGICAL FALLACIES

4.2

CHAPTER

It is the mark of an educated mind to be able to entertain a thought without accepting it.

Aristotle

Leading experts in the field of critical thinking captured the public's attention by stating the obvious: "Teachers are able to foster critical thinking only to the extent that they themselves think critically" (Paul & Elder, 2007, p. 5). In fact, Paul and Elder went on to assert that teachers' deficiencies in critical thinking skills "may be the single most significant barrier to student achievement of critical thinking competencies" (p. 5).

How can one model a competency that he does not possess? He cannot. Undeniably, a preservice teacher's professional development and proficiency in critical thinking is of vital importance—not only for themselves but for the students who they will eventually teach.

OBJECTIVES

The learner will:

- identify and explain the term *logical fallacy*;
- identify, explain, and locate examples of at least 12 common logical fallacies; and
- analyze arguments in blogs, editorials, news articles, or other forms of public discourse and to identify.

It is not enough to simply list types of logical fallacies and provide examples. It is of greater importance that one develops habits of logical thinking that do not succumb to logical fallacies. By developing basic proficiency in detecting logical fallacies, an educator will become a more adept problem solver. By so doing, the educator will become a role model for students. In turn, those students will learn how to think critically and effectively use logic to make decisions and solve problems.

VIGNETTE

"Our Parent–Teacher Association's fall fund-raiser is a waste of time because they are all just a bunch of meddling moms."

What is your initial response to that comment? Did you think, "Yeah, the speaker's right. PTA moms really do meddle in the school's business," or did you ask, "Why is the speaker stereotyping all members of the PTA, and what relevance does that have to the PTA's programs?"

The logical fallacy committed by this speaker is appropriately labeled an "ad hominem" attack. Instead of providing substantive evidence to support his position that the fall fund-raiser is a waste of time, the speaker attacked the character of all of the individuals who belong to the PTA.

Preservice teachers must become proficient critical thinkers, so let's explore some of the most common logical fallacies preservice teachers may unwittingly employ or eventually encounter in the field of education.

Types of Logical Fallacies

Ad hominem and tu quoque

Ad populum

Appeal to authority

Begging the claim/question

Circular argument

False cause (post hoc ergo propter hoc)

False dichotomy (either/or)

Genetic fallacy

Hasty generalization

Loaded question

Missing the point

Moral equivalence

Red herring

Slippery slope

Straw man

This list of common terms is by no means exhaustive. There are additional types of logical fallacies, and as you develop your skills of analysis and critical thinking, you will begin to detect those logical fallacies even in everyday conversations.

WEBCONNECT

Using only .edu websites or critical thinking.org, locate definitions and examples for at least 12 of the aforementioned logical fallacies. As you do so, fill out the template below entitled "The Dirty Dozen."

EXERCISE: COMPLETE THE CHART BELOW, FOLLOWING THE EXAMPLE PROVIDED

"The Dirty Dozen"

Name of logical fallacy	Description of the nature of the fallacy	Example (provided by the source)
Hasty generalization	An assumption one makes based upon insufficient evidence or biased information	"Even though it's only the first day, I can tell this is going to be a boring course." (OWL Purdue, 2014)

EXERCISE: PRESENTATION

Develop a presentation (using one of the following or a combination thereof) which will assist you in committing these precepts to memory:

- Mnemonic device
- Hand gestures or body movements
- Poem, rap, or cheer
- Visual representation

You may complete this exercise with a partner or small group.

LET'S TALK

Share your presentation with other groups. Provide positive feedback to each group regarding the most memorable portion(s) of their presentation.

EXERCISE: CREATE A QUIZ

With a partner, create a quiz that requires learners to match the name of a logical fallacy with its corresponding definition. Prepare two copies of the quiz for the exchange in class.

EXERCISE: TAKE A QUIZ

Exchange quizzes with members of other groups and complete the quiz individually.

THINK AND WRITE

Summarize your progress toward identifying and explaining at least a dozen types of logical fallacies. Of all of the logical fallacies you've studied, which are you most inclined to commit?

Now that you have committed some of these logical fallacies to memory, let's locate examples of these logical fallacies in public discourse.

🌐 WEBCONNECT

Search blogs and online editorials for additional examples of logical fallacies.

🗂 EXERCISE: COLLECTOR

As you encounter discussions of educational policy and practices (local, state, and national scene), become a "collector" of the logical fallacies that pepper the landscape of educational discourse. For example, arguments for and against the following contemporary issues invariably include logical fallacies perpetuated by one or both sides. By analyzing and collecting flawed arguments for and against issues, you will become a more adept teacher leader who can contribute to addressing and solving the challenges educators face in the twenty-first century.

Here is a list of a small portion of the controversial issues in education today:

1. Adoption of national curriculum/common core
2. Bilingual education
3. Homeschooling
4. Measures to prevent school shootings
5. School vouchers
6. Same-sex classrooms
7. Merit pay for teachers
8. Technology in the classroom
9. Year-round schooling

🗂 EXERCISE: AS YOU COMPLETE THE CHART BELOW, USE THIS GUIDE TO COMPLETE THE CHART CORRECTLY.

Column One: Write out the educational topic you encountered (in a journal or newspaper article, class discussion, conversation in the field, etc.).

Column Two: Summarize the controversy.

Column Three: Summarize the logical fallacy perpetuated by one (or both) of the parties.

Column Four: Identify the type of logical fallacy that it is.

Topic of discussion	Controversial issue (each topic may include multiple)	Logical fallacy committed	Type of logical fallacy
Schools of choice	Should parents be free to send children to school districts in which they do not live?	If you were a true American, you would support every person's right to choose a school.	Ad populum

Logical Fallacies in Educational Arenas

Topic of discussion	Controversial issue (each topic may include multiple)	Logical fallacy committed	Type of logical fallacy

(See Appendix for additional glossary pages.)

EXERCISE

Compose an essay in editorial fashion rebutting one of the editorials or blogs that committed one or more logical fallacies. Tactfully address the flawed logic and explain why the logic is flawed.

THINK AND WRITE

What are the most valuable insights you gleaned from this lesson? Share three to five insights in a bulleted list.

LEADERSHIP: FOUR CENTRAL COMPETENCIES

5
CHAPTER

Teaching and leading are distinguishable occupations, but every great leader is clearly teaching—and every great teacher is leading.

John W. Gardner

Implicit in any construct of leadership theory is that leaders cannot exist without willing followers. Examined in the context of teaching, that presumes that teachers are not leaders simply because students are assigned to their classrooms or care. Teachers become *teacher leaders* when their students respect them—not because the students *must* follow but because the students have chosen to follow the teacher's leadership.

For decades—if not centuries—the question of whether leaders are born or made has been pondered. Bennis and Thomas (2007) interviewed successful leaders from two American generations: the Boomers and the Gen Xers/Yers. The interviewers concluded that—regardless of age, race, gender, ethnicity, or era—successful leaders emerged victorious from crucible experiences. Each one of those leaders persisted through adversity by virtue of four competencies that were "central to their ability to lead" (p. 9):

- adaptive capacity,
- the ability to engage others through shared meaning,
- a distinctive and compelling voice, and
- unshakeable integrity (p. 9).

Reframing those four competencies into the context of the field of teaching, I postulate that the equivalencies of these capacities are properly labeled as follows:

- flexibility and resilience,
- inspiration and motivation,
- "teacher presence," and
- integrity and competence.

This chapter begins with the assumption that effective leaders demonstrate proficiency in the fundamental skills previously addressed in this textbook: oral communication, human interaction, and critical thinking. Therefore, the fundamentals of each skill need not be revisited. Instead, this chapter focuses upon the four central competencies that empower a professional educator to become a teacher leader.

OBJECTIVES

The learner will:

- develop an understanding of the terms *adaptive capacity*, *crucible*, and *consensus* as they are used in the field of education;
- identify and explain the four central competencies of effective leadership;
- reflect upon previous experiences that relate to the four central competencies of effective leadership; and
- self-assess proficiency in the four central competencies of effective leadership.

FLEXIBILITY AND RESILIENCE

Effective leaders ooze confidence—not the sort of confidence that is readily detected as false bravado or arrogance, but an authentic, can-do confidence that was born out of adversity. In the face of crucible experiences that test one's mettle and challenge one's values, a leader discovers that they have "what it takes" to survive—if not thrive—in the face of adversity. For teacher leaders, crucible experiences empower them to take initiative, assume leadership, and respond to varied situations confidently. With self-confidence, the teacher leader is not threatened by others who may take initiative or bring forth brilliance. Instead, teacher leaders surround themselves with others who may be more talented or intelligent than they are, and they seek to empower others who have not yet found their voice or stride.

In the context of the classroom, the teacher leader is willing to take risks to advance student learning. They embrace roadblocks, schedule changes, and snow days. They view difficult conversations as opportunities to win over parents or colleagues, and they view reticent students as the most desirable of challenges. Teacher leaders believe in themselves, and they believe in others.

THINK AND WRITE

Recall and retell a crucible experience in your life that revealed to you that you have the "mettle" to make it in life—and perhaps even in this career of teaching.

LET'S TALK

Share excerpts of the crucible experience you recorded, and brainstorm ways that the lessons learned from that crucible experience can be applied to your success as a teacher leader.

 LET'S TALK

"[Teacher leaders] embrace reports of head lice, politics-as-usual, cranky colleagues, and schedule disruptions as 'all in a day's work.' They view difficult conversations as opportunities to win over parents or colleagues, and reticent or resistant students as the most desirable of all challenges." What is the author's point? Make reference to the four central competencies as you discuss your thoughts.

ABILITY TO INSPIRE AND MOTIVATE

> *"The mediocre teacher tells. The good teacher explains. The superior teacher demonstrates. The great teacher inspires."*

> William Arthur Ward

Perhaps one of my all-time favorite "teacher quotes," this observation has guided and challenged my teaching practices for two decades. You, as a teacher leader, are embarking upon a similar journey, and I trust this reminds you of what teacher leaders do so well: they inspire.

 LET'S TALK

Recall and retell a time in your K-12 experience when a teacher inspired you. Explain how that teacher did so. Brainstorm how this technique or another technique may serve you well as you strive to inspire your own students.

TEACHER PRESENCE

The effective teacher leader is a magnificent communicator who engages followers and is perceived as authentic and credible. Bennis and Thomas (2007) describe this engaging form of presence as a "distinctive and compelling voice." Perhaps this voice could be viewed as persona, a distinctive revelation of the leader's character. Cashman (2008) acknowledges that many leaders develop a persona as a leader, and he suggests that persona is not problematic so long as it is not a façade but rooted in strong moral character.

 ## LET'S TALK

Have you begun to develop or reveal your teaching persona yet? Share with a partner what you perceive your persona to be, and when you began to notice or develop it in the context of leading children and others.

 ## LET'S TALK

Consider for a moment that the word "discipline" is made up of the word "disciple," and a disciple is someone who follows willingly. Now apply that insight when brainstorming with a partner your response to the following question: "What is the difference between a teacher leader and a teacher dictator? Explain."

INTEGRITY AND COMPETENCE

Effective teacher leaders are trusting and trustworthy. They evoke and maintain trust in the classroom and greater community. As *trust* is the nominative word in both of the preceding sentences, it is important to pause to examine a definition of trust that is highly esteemed in the leadership community.

"Trust is a function of both character and competence" (Covey, 2006, p. 25). According to renowned leadership expert Stephen M. R. Covey (2006), any leadership failure is the outcome of one of the following: lack of trust or lack of competence.

 ## LET'S TALK

Reread Covey's definition of trust. How do teachers establish trust? Generate a list of behaviors that provide evidence of teacher competence, along with a list of behaviors that build trust among students, teachers, and families.

 **LET'S TALK**

With a partner, read and interpret each of the following quotes, and then select two that you would be willing to commit to memory:

> *"The most important thing to have in mind is that leaders need followers."*
> John Gardner

> *"Trust is a function of both character and competence."*
> Stephen M. R. Covey

> *"That which we are, we shall teach, not voluntarily, but involuntarily."*
> Ralph Waldo Emerson

> *"If wisdom's ways you would wisely seek, these five things observe with care: Of whom you speak, to whom you speak, how, when, and where."*
> The McGuffey Reader

> *"If one had to name a single, all-purpose instrument of leadership, it would be communication."*
> John Gardner

> *"The mediocre teacher tells. The good teacher explains. The superior teacher demonstrates. The great teacher inspires."*
> William Arthur Ward

EXERCISE: SELF-ASSESS YOUR CURRENT BEHAVIORS IN RELATION TO THE COMPETENCIES OF TEACHER LEADERS

Complete the following self-assessment:

COMPETENCIES OF TEACHER LEADERS	FREQUENCY			
	Rarely/never	*Occasionally*	*Frequently*	*Always*
Flexibility				
Resilience				
Ability to inspire				
Ability to motivate				
"Teacher presence"				
Integrity				
Competence				

📝 THINK AND WRITE

Which competencies of a teacher leader do you possess in the greatest measure at this time? Explain.

📝 THINK AND WRITE

In which areas must I make the greatest gains before I lead in my own classroom some day? Explain.

We say that we want effective leadership; but Hitler was effective.
Criteria beyond effectiveness are needed.

John W. Gardner

Reality check: Teachers wield power—tremendous power. Students of all ages are wittingly or unwittingly influenced by their teachers. Students follow and trust these prominent role models in their lives. And the vast majority of teachers steward that powerful relationship exceedingly well. However, when teachers abuse their power and violate students' trust, lives are harmed and the reputation of our noble profession is sullied.

Therefore, teacher educators strive to nurture the professional development of preservice teachers who will soon become the moral agents in their respective schools. Though strong, ethical administrators are vital to the wellness of an educational community, administrators alone cannot and do not make all of the judgment calls that are required each day. The purpose of this lesson is to guide the preservice teacher into decision-making practices that adhere to the Educator's Code of Ethics and empower the preservice teacher to wisely wield the power they will be given as professionals.

OBJECTIVES

The learner will:

- reflect upon the effect of their professional decisions and actions on students and others in the learning community;
- practice and refine leadership skills when discussing ethical dilemmas; and
- reflect upon self-assessment and peer assessment of practice performances.

LET'S TALK

Make reference to the introductory comments in this lesson as you contemplate the following metaphor:

"On the highway of life, teachers are the 'big rigs.'"
Sally Ingles

In small groups, use the following prompts to guide your discussions:

1. Discuss the influence of semitruck trailers (relative to the smaller cars, trucks, and motorcycles which they encounter) on the flow of traffic on interstate highways across the United States.
2. Consider the impact of the errors that a semitruck may make as compared with the impact of errors made by a motorcyclist.
3. Draw connections between big rigs on the highway of life with teachers on the "road of life."

THINK AND WRITE

Write a brief reflection of the powerful role you will wield as a teacher and of the effect your professional decisions and actions will have upon students and others in the learning community.

Codes of Ethics

In Chapter 1, Lesson 4, you located codes of ethics for teachers from state and national sources and analyzed the contents of each. You articulated the guiding principles common to these various sources and examined teacher scandals that fly in the face of adherence to codes of ethics.

How can this be? Are teachers not aware of the codes of ethics espoused at all levels of government? Are teachers indifferent to these honor codes that were written to guide moral behavior? Perhaps you've already reached your own conclusion on the matter. The problem is not that we lack leadership in schools; the problem is that we lack *ethical* leadership in schools. Teachers—not just administrators—are leaders in schools, and all teachers need to lead by making ethical decisions.

📝 THINK AND WRITE

"Leadership is not something we do . . . It is an expression of who we are" (Cashman, 2008, p. 18). What are your initial thoughts when you read this quote? Suggest a connection between public leadership and personal integrity. Is it likely that someone who lacks personal integrity will lead with professional integrity? Explain.

Guidelines for *Ethical* Behavior in the Classroom

Professional educators consistently adhere to the NEA Code of Ethics for Professional Educators. In a sentence: they do no harm. Community members can count on ethical teacher leaders because these teachers are men and women of their word. They are honest, never slanderous, and they follow through with commitments they make.

Even when subjected to personal attacks from parents or others, ethical teacher leaders do not respond. They refuse to speak ill of their students, their students' families, administrators, paraprofessionals, and other support staff. They resist gossip, squelch slander, and never physically or emotionally harm the children they serve.

Guidelines for *Leadership* Behavior in the Classroom

Now that we have established the absolute necessity that teacher leaders are ethical leaders, let us focus our attention to behaviors that constitute effective leadership skill.

🗂 EXERCISE: BEHAVIOR INDICATORS: LEADERSHIP

As you prepare to engage in these consensus-building exercises, it is vital that you carefully review the following:

1. The operative definition of consensus for these exercises
2. The behavior indicators of effective leadership skills

Operative Definition of Consensus

"We have arrived at consensus when all points of view have been heard, and the will of the group is evident—even to those who most oppose it." (Rick DuFour, 2008)

Leadership Skills

Behavior Indicators: Leadership

	ACCEPTABLE	NEEDS IMPROVEMENT
Self-assured	Eye contact, posture, and tone of voice demonstrate confidence; willing to take risks; resilient	Poor eye contact and posture; shaky voice or hesitation in voice; unwilling to take a risk or try again after failure; timid Overly confident; arrogant; aloof
Takes initiative	"Jumps in" or offers to contribute to the completion of a task or to fill in when there is need	Holds back; does not start or take charge of any portion of any task "Jumps in" or takes charge of *every* task
Provides direction for group	Notices when the group may be faltering or wandering off task; intervenes in a non-threatening way that cajoles the group back on track	Follower only; does not assume responsibility to lead at any juncture of group collaborations Domineering; attempts to control the group instead of lead the group
"Presence"; others seem to listen or defer to him/her	Earns the trust and respect of others—whether by exuding charisma, projecting confidence, or demonstrating competence	Others seem unconvinced of, aversive to, or indifferent to his or her direction (or lack thereof)
Empowers others	Inspires; motivates; encourages others to contribute and/or use their gifts	Gives no indication that s/he notices or cares about others' contributions to the group

 **LET'S TALK**

In small groups, discuss your observations of the two items you just reviewed. Seek out clarification from classmates and instructor before continuing on to the next exercise.

ASSESSMENT PREPARATION

Before you complete each of the following exercises, determine which of the following means of peer assessment you will use for each activity. The "Behavior Indicators: Leadership Skills" form will be used for both peer assessment and self-assessment.

Peer Assessment Options

1. Groups Take Turns

   With this option, each small group of students collaborates in a "fish bowl" sort of approach. The group that collaborates is in the center of the room. Classmates observe from the outside of the circle and complete the peer assessment form for their assigned partner.

2. Designated Videographers

   Depending upon class size, a different group of students is deemed "videographer crew" for each exercise. Each of those students is assigned to digitally record one small group's collaborative session. For example, in a class size of 15, the instructor could establish three groups of four students. Each of the remaining students would be assigned one group to digitally record the collaborative exercise. The videographer role would change for every exercise.

Now is the time for you to begin practicing your leadership skills as you strive for consensus on the following ethical dilemmas.

Peer-Assessor: Behavior Indicators: Leadership Skills

Speaker's Name _____ Date _____

Peer Assessor's Name _____ Date _____

Leadership Skills

Behavior Indicators: Leadership

	ACCEPTABLE	NEEDS IMPROVEMENT
Self-assured	Eye contact, posture, and tone of voice demonstrate confidence; willing to take risks; resilient	Poor eye contact and posture; shaky voice or hesitation in voice; unwilling to take a risk or try again after failure; timid Overly confident; arrogant; aloof
Takes initiative	"Jumps in" or offers to contribute to the completion of a task or to fill in when there is need	Holds back; does not start or take charge of any portion of any task "Jumps in" or takes charge of *every* task
Provides direction for group	Notices when the group may be faltering or wandering off task; intervenes in a non-threatening way that cajoles the group back on track	Follower only; does not assume responsibility to lead at any juncture of group collaborations Domineering; attempts to control the group instead of lead the group
"Presence"; others seem to listen or defer to him/her	Earns the trust and respect of others—whether by exuding charisma, projecting confidence, or demonstrating competence	Others seem unconvinced of, aversive to, or indifferent to his or her direction (or lack thereof)
Empowers others	Inspires; motivates; encourages others to contribute and/or use their gifts	Gives no indication that s/he notices or cares about others' contributions to the group

📑 EXERCISE: CASE STUDY #1

Imagine that you are a nontenured teacher who has been asked by your administrator to lie to the Board of Education. Will you lie? What values are in conflict here? What ethical principles are at stake? What is your group's consensus on the matter? You have 20 minutes to reach consensus.

Self-Assessment: Behavior Indicators: Leadership Skills
(if a digital recording was made)

Speaker's Name _____ Date _____

Leadership Skills

Self-Assessment: Behavior Indicators: Leadership

	ACCEPTABLE	NEEDS IMPROVEMENT
Self-assured	Eye contact, posture, and tone of voice demonstrate confidence; willing to take risks; resilient	Poor eye contact and posture; shaky voice or hesitation in voice; unwilling to take a risk or try again after failure; timid Overly confident; arrogant; aloof
Takes initiative	"Jumps in" or offers to contribute to the completion of a task or to fill in when there is need	Holds back; does not start or take charge of any portion of any task "Jumps in" or takes charge of *every* task
Provides direction for group	Notices when the group may be faltering or wandering off task; intervenes in a nonthreatening way that cajoles the group back on track	Follower only; does not assume responsibility to lead at any juncture of group collaborations Domineering; attempts to control the group instead of lead the group
"Presence"; others seem to listen or defer to him/her	Earns the trust and respect of others—whether by exuding charisma, projecting confidence, or demonstrating competence	Others seem unconvinced of, aversive to, or indifferent to his or her direction (or lack thereof)
Empowers others	Inspires; motivates; encourages others to contribute and/or use their gifts	Gives no indication that s/he notices or cares about others' contributions to the group

Leadership Skills

Peer-Assessment: Behavior Indicators: Leadership

	ACCEPTABLE	NEEDS IMPROVEMENT
Self-assured	Eye contact, posture, and tone of voice demonstrate confidence; willing to take risks; resilient	Poor eye contact and posture; shaky voice or hesitation in voice; unwilling to take a risk or try again after failure; timid Overly confident; arrogant; aloof
Takes initiative	"Jumps in" or offers to contribute to the completion of a task or to fill in when there is need	Holds back; does not start or take charge of any portion of any task "Jumps in" or takes charge of *every* task
Provides direction for group	Notices when the group may be faltering or wandering off task; intervenes in a non-threatening way that cajoles the group back on track	Follower only; does not assume responsibility to lead at any juncture of group collaborations Domineering; attempts to control the group instead of lead the group
"Presence"; others seem to listen or defer to him/her	Earns the trust and respect of others—whether by exuding charisma, projecting confidence, or demonstrating competence	Others seem unconvinced of, aversive to, or indifferent to his or her direction (or lack thereof)
Empowers others	Inspires; motivates; encourages others to contribute and/ or use their gifts	Gives no indication that s/he notices or cares about others' contributions to the group

📝 THINK AND WRITE

In one sentence, clearly state whether or not you will lie to the Board of Education. Following that direct statement, include two to three paragraphs in which you justify your decision by making direct reference to guidelines from your state's or the NEA's Code of Ethics.

🗐 EXERCISE: CASE STUDY #2

Imagine that you are high school teacher who notices that one of your students (a graduating senior) is behaving erratically—in a manner that suggests he may be under the influence of alcohol. If you report your suspicion to administration and your suspicion is verified, this student will not be able to march in the upcoming graduation ceremony. This student comes from a highly esteemed family in the community that wields power over the school administration and local school board. Your annual performance evaluation may be negatively affected if you report this student. Will you report your suspicion to administration? What values are in conflict here? What ethical principles are at stake? What is your group's consensus on the matter? You have 20 minutes to reach consensus.

**Self-Assessment: Behavior Indicators: Leadership Skills
(if a digital recording was made)**

Speaker's Name _____ Date _____

Leadership Skills

Self-Assessment: Behavior Indicators: Leadership

	ACCEPTABLE	NEEDS IMPROVEMENT
Self-assured	Eye contact, posture, and tone of voice demonstrate confidence; willing to take risks; resilient	Poor eye contact and posture; shaky voice or hesitation in voice; unwilling to take a risk or try again after failure; timid Overly confident; arrogant; aloof
Takes initiative	"Jumps in" or offers to contribute to the completion of a task or to fill in when there is need	Holds back; does not start or take charge of any portion of any task "Jumps in" or takes charge of *every* task
Provides direction for group	Notices when the group may be faltering or wandering off task; intervenes in a non-threatening way that cajoles the group back on track	Follower only; does not assume responsibility to lead at any juncture of group collaborations Domineering; attempts to control the group instead of lead the group
"Presence"; others seem to listen or defer to him/her	Earns the trust and respect of others—whether by exuding charisma, projecting confidence, or demonstrating competence	Others seem unconvinced of, aversive to, or indifferent to his or her direction (or lack thereof)
Empowers others	Inspires; motivates; encourages others to contribute and/or use their gifts	Gives no indication that s/he notices or cares about others' contributions to the group

Leadership Skills

Peer-Assessment: Behavior Indicators: Leadership

	ACCEPTABLE	NEEDS IMPROVEMENT
Self-assured	Eye contact, posture, and tone of voice demonstrate confidence; willing to take risks; resilient	Poor eye contact and posture; shaky voice or hesitation in voice; unwilling to take a risk or try again after failure; timid Overly confident; arrogant; aloof
Takes initiative	"Jumps in" or offers to contribute to the completion of a task or to fill in when there is need	Holds back; does not start or take charge of any portion of any task "Jumps in" or takes charge of *every* task
Provides direction for group	Notices when the group may be faltering or wandering off task; intervenes in a non-threatening way that cajoles the group back on track	Follower only; does not assume responsibility to lead at any juncture of group collaborations Domineering; attempts to control the group instead of lead the group
"Presence"; others seem to listen or defer to him/her	Earns the trust and respect of others—whether by exuding charisma, projecting confidence, or demonstrating competence	Others seem unconvinced of, aversive to, or indifferent to his or her direction (or lack thereof)
Empowers others	Inspires; motivates; encourages others to contribute and/or use their gifts	Gives no indication that s/he notices or cares about others' contributions to the group

📝 THINK AND WRITE

In one sentence, clearly state whether or not you will report your suspicion to administration. Following that definitive response include two to three paragraphs in which you justify your decision by making direct reference to guidelines from your state's or the NEA's Code of Ethics.

📝 THINK AND WRITE

Compare the peer assessment feedback you received with your self-assessments. In which areas do you demonstrate the greatest competency? In which areas must you continue to strive and grow?

PUTTING IT ALL TOGETHER

6
CHAPTER

Confidence is the result of hours and days and weeks and years of constant work and dedication.

Roger Staubach

Whether participating in a staff meeting, conversing with a parent, or interviewing for a teaching position, a professional educator must adeptly employ oral communication skills, interpersonal skills, critical thinking skills, and leadership skills. In previous chapters, we refined those skills in relative isolation of one another. In this chapter, we employ all simultaneously as we simulate real-life teaching situations via panel discussions and mock teacher interviews.

OBJECTIVES

The learner will:

- practice and refine oral communication, human interaction, critical thinking, and leadership skills in the context of a collegial conversation;
- self-assess proficiency in oral communication, human interaction, critical thinking, and leadership skills in the context of a collegial conversation; and
- reflect upon self-assessment and peer assessment of practice performances.

PANEL DISCUSSIONS

Panel discussions are small group discussions in which participants engage in authentic conversation with one another. Very often, the discussions center upon questions of ethics and proper courses of action regarding contemporary education issues. These interactions are designed to heighten preservice teachers' critical thinking skills and prepare students to become future teacher leaders on curriculum committees, in staff meetings, and advocates of sound educational practices on local, state, and national levels.

The beauty of the panel discussion is that all voices must be heard. As opposed to classroom discussions that so often digress into a teacher monologue or a conversation among a teacher and a few students, the panel discussion places the onus for discussion squarely on the shoulders of four to five students at a time. The panelists' chairs are arranged in a half-circle at the front of the room, so that participants are primarily facing one another and then—to a lesser extent—the remaining classroom audience. Participants are given an amount of time (perhaps 8–10 minutes) to discuss a prescribed portion of the assigned reading the week, the completed assignment that was brought to class, or the students' observations during field experience.

Panelists are encouraged to make reference to their assigned reading and completed assignment to guide their thinking, but they are never allowed to simply read from their assignment during a panel discussion.

Before engaging in a panel discussion, participants need to learn and follow guidelines of interaction that will maximize efficiency, facilitate healthy discussion, and foster positive working relationships among participants. The following guidelines are included to assist preservice teachers in achieving those ends.

GUIDING PRINCIPLES OF COLLEGIAL CONVERSATION

1. Practice Common Courtesy

   Be vigilant in the use of the most common graces of "please," "thank you," and "excuse me" as needed. If you interrupt someone while they are speaking, immediately apologize and ask them to continue with what they were saying.

   Example: "I'm sorry, Susan. What were you saying?" or "I'm sorry to have interrupted you, Susan. Please continue."

   a. **Filter.** Is it true? Is it kind? Is it necessary?

      Sometimes that which we share with others is constructive feedback. A vital question to ask yourself before doing so is can you make the comment in such a way that it is tactfully spoken in a spirit of love and concern?

      Example: "I notice that you have several questions on this subject. Will you please choose the one or two questions you need answered now, and write down the rest? I want to make certain that your classmates also have an opportunity to ask questions during class."

   b. **Share the air.** In a collegial conversation, we make certain that our thoughts and queries do not monopolize the group's time.

      Example: "I've already shared why I feel strongly about this. Susan, what are your thoughts on the subject?"

   c. **Disagree Agreeably.** Share a differing viewpoint without being cantankerous.

      It is acceptable to hold a differing opinion, but do not attack a person or insult the speaker (eye rolling, aggressive language) because you disagree with his or her ideas.

      Example: "I can see how you reached that conclusion. Another way of looking at this is . . . ."

      In that same vein, be gracious when others challenge or refute your positions. Do not interpret it as a personal attack.

2. **"Move the Ball down the Field"**

   To use a football metaphor, some lateral passes are acceptable, but forward passes are preferred. In other words, we want forward progress.

   It is only natural for learners to attempt to assimilate or accommodate new information by connecting new material to previous learning and personal experiences. Such behavior is very important for the learner to continue. Keep doing so . . . but carefully select which personal connections you share with the group and which are to be used for your own edification. In other words, when you encounter new concepts over the course of a discussion, ask yourself four questions:

- Which of my previous experiences relate to this topic?
- Of all of those experiences, which seems most germane to this discussion?
- Would the sharing of this experience be valuable to several others in the group?
- Do we have enough time to complete the task at hand if I share this experience?

Example: "I encountered the same situation when I completed my student teaching. I concur with your conclusion on this matter."

3. **Contribute; Don't Coast**

Collaboration is a group effort—not the exercise of a few extroverts who are eager to share their own thoughts and ideas.

Coasting is marked by extended silence, and perhaps the occasional contribution I call "chiming in."

Example of "Chiming In": "I agree with everything you guys said. It's all great. Just great."

Example of Contributing: "Perhaps another thing worth mentioning is that . . ." or "Though I agree with _____ , I take exception to _____ ."

4. **Speak Up**

When a colleague's contribution is inaccurate or unclear, a gentle correction or a request for clarification is warranted.

Example: "I'm sorry, Shea. I didn't follow that. Will you please explain that again?"

Example: "You mentioned _____ . Will you expound upon that further? I'm not certain that I understand you correctly on this point."

Example: "I understand what you are saying, but I interpreted that differently. My understanding is that . . ."

THINK AND WRITE

Which of the aforementioned guidelines do you seem to follow with the greatest regularity? Which are likely your greatest areas for growth?

▶ SHOW ME: "PANEL DISCUSSION"

View an instructor introducing the "Panel Discussion" exercise to students followed by her students' first attempts at effectively participating in one. Use the "Panel Discussion Rubric" to assess one of the members of the panel in the demonstration video. Make certain that each person in your class is evaluating at least one individual in the video. (One rubric follows here. Additional rubrics are available in the "Appendices" section in the back of the book.)

Panel Discussion Rubric   **Participant's Name:** _____

3	2	1	0	Skill	Standard Peer Evaluator's Name: _____
				Oral communication	When speaking, the student • demonstrates good eye contact and assertive, engaged body language; • uses standard English (grammar/usage/word choice) appropriately; • projects voice clearly with appropriate volume, inflection, and fluency; and • conveys ideas with precision (gets to the point) and clarity (easy to follow). Comments:
				Human interaction	When listening and/or responding to others, the student • acknowledges the speaker with appropriate eye contact and engaged body language; • shows tact when engaging others in conversation, acknowledges others' contributions; • builds rapport by demonstrating supportiveness, warmth, and/or humor; and • refrains from monopolizing talk time. Comments:
				Critical thinking	Student contributions • are thorough and logical; • are clear and organized; • make reference to big ideas, underlying principles, and/or essential questions; and • include insightful questions or questions for clarification as needed. Comments:

3	2	1	0	Skill	Standard Peer Evaluator's Name: _____
				Evidence of preparation and comprehension	The student demonstrates • accurate comprehension of the assigned reading and discussion questions; • evidence of preparation by making reference to assigned reading; and • evidence of preparation by making no fewer than two substantive contributions. Comments:

Levels of proficiency: 3 = Above average, 2 = Average, 1 = Below average, and 0 = Not observed.

LET'S TALK

In small groups, discuss individual performances in the demo video in relation to the "Panel Discussion Rubric." In which categories did individuals demonstrate the greatest proficiency? In which areas do these participants in the demonstration video need to make the most gains?

 THINK AND WRITE

Based upon performance behavior, with which of the individuals in the demonstration video do you most identify? Compare your perceived proficiencies with his or her. What can you learn from his or her performance to improve your own?

Before you complete each of the following exercises, determine which of the following means of peer assessment you will use for each activity. The Panel Discussion Rubric will be used for both peer assessment and self-assessment.

PEER ASSESSMENT OPTIONS

1. Groups Take Turns

    With this option, each small group of students collaborates in a "fish bowl" sort of approach. The group that collaborates is in the center of the room. Classmates observe from the outside of the circle and complete the peer-assessment form for their assigned partner.

2. Designated Videographers

    Depending upon class size, a different group of students is deemed "videographer crew" for each exercise. Each of those students is assigned to digitally record one small group's collaborative session. For example, in a class size of 15, the instructor could establish three groups of four students. Each of the remaining students would be assigned one group to digitally record the collaborative exercise. The videographer role would change for every exercise.

3. Instructor Preference

Now is the time for you to begin practicing your skills in collegial conversation. For these initial panel discussions, your instructor may use the following prompts. However, future panel discussions may be based upon other assigned readings, observations, and assignments completed for this instructor.

Peer Assessor to Complete

Panel Discussion Rubric   **Participant's Name:** _____

3	2	1	0	Skill	Standard Peer Evaluator's Name: _____
				Oral communication	When speaking, the student • demonstrates good eye contact and assertive, engaged body language; • uses standard English (grammar/usage/word choice) appropriately; • projects voice clearly with appropriate volume, inflection, and fluency; and • conveys ideas with precision (gets to the point) and clarity (easy to follow). Comments:
				Human interaction	When listening and/or responding to others, the student • acknowledges the speaker with appropriate eye contact and engaged body language; • shows tact when engaging others in conversation, acknowledges others' contributions; • builds rapport by demonstrating supportiveness, warmth, and/or humor; and • refrains from monopolizing talk time. Comments:
				Critical thinking	Student contributions • are thorough and logical; • are clear and organized; • make reference to big ideas, underlying principles, and/or essential questions; and • include insightful questions or questions for clarification as needed. Comments:

3	2	1	0	Skill	Standard Peer Evaluator's Name: _____
				Evidence of preparation and comprehension	The student demonstrates • accurate comprehension of the assigned reading and discussion questions; • evidence of preparation by making reference to assigned reading; and • evidence of preparation by making no fewer than two substantive contributions. Comments:
Levels of proficiency: 3 = Above average, 2 = Average, 1 = Below average, and 0 = Not observed.					

EXERCISE: PANEL DISCUSSION #1

What is the most important message you should convey to your students each day? In what ways, other than verbalizing that message, can you convey it?

Self-Assessment (if a digital recording of the performance was made)

Panel Discussion Rubric   Participant's Name: _____

3	2	1	0	Skill	Standard Peer Evaluator's Name: _____
				Oral communication	When speaking, the student • demonstrates good eye contact and assertive, engaged body language; • uses standard English (grammar/usage/word choice) appropriately; • projects voice clearly with appropriate volume, inflection, and fluency; and • conveys ideas with precision (gets to the point) and clarity (easy to follow). Comments:
				Human interaction	When listening and/or responding to others, the student • acknowledges the speaker with appropriate eye contact and engaged body language; • shows tact when engaging others in conversation, acknowledges others' contributions; • builds rapport by demonstrating supportiveness, warmth, and/or humor; and • refrains from monopolizing talk time. Comments:
				Critical thinking	Student contributions • are thorough and logical; • are clear and organized; • make reference to big ideas, underlying principles, and/or essential questions; and • include insightful questions or questions for clarification as needed. Comments:

3	2	1	0	Skill	Standard Peer Evaluator's Name: _____
				Evidence of preparation and comprehension	The student demonstrates <ul><li>accurate comprehension of the assigned reading and discussion questions;</li><li>evidence of preparation by making reference to assigned reading; and</li><li>evidence of preparation by making no fewer than two substantive contributions.</li></ul>Comments:
Levels of proficiency: 3 = Above average, 2 = Average, 1 = Below average, and 0 = Not observed.

Peer Assessor to Complete for the Next Panel Discussion

Panel Discussion Rubric   **Participant's Name:** _____

3	2	1	0	Skill	Standard Peer Evaluator's Name: _____
				Oral communication	When speaking, the student • demonstrates good eye contact and assertive, engaged body language; • uses standard English (grammar/usage/word choice) appropriately; • projects voice clearly with appropriate volume, inflection, and fluency; and • conveys ideas with precision (gets to the point) and clarity (easy to follow). Comments:
				Human interaction	When listening and/or responding to others, the student • acknowledges the speaker with appropriate eye contact and engaged body language; • shows tact when engaging others in conversation, acknowledges others' contributions; • builds rapport by demonstrating supportiveness, warmth, and/or humor; and • refrains from monopolizing talk time. Comments:
				Critical thinking	Student contributions • are thorough and logical; • are clear and organized; • make reference to big ideas, underlying principles, and/or essential questions; and • include insightful questions or questions for clarification as needed. Comments:

3	2	1	0	Skill	Standard Peer Evaluator's Name: _____
				Evidence of preparation and comprehension	The student demonstrates • accurate comprehension of the assigned reading and discussion questions; • evidence of preparation by making reference to assigned reading; and • evidence of preparation by making no fewer than two substantive contributions. Comments:

Levels of proficiency: 3 = Above average, 2 = Average, 1 = Below average, and 0 = Not observed.

EXERCISE: PANEL DISCUSSION #2

What are the three most vital characteristics of the effective teacher?

Student to Complete as Self-Assessment
(if a digital recording of the performance was made)

Panel Discussion Rubric   Participant's Name: _____

3	2	1	0	Skill	Standard Peer Evaluator's Name: _____
				Oral communication	When speaking, the student • demonstrates good eye contact and assertive, engaged body language; • uses standard English (grammar/usage/word choice) appropriately; • projects voice clearly with appropriate volume, inflection, and fluency; and • conveys ideas with precision (gets to the point) and clarity (easy to follow). Comments:
				Human interaction	When listening and/or responding to others, the student • acknowledges the speaker with appropriate eye contact and engaged body language; • shows tact when engaging others in conversation, acknowledges others' contributions; • builds rapport by demonstrating supportiveness, warmth, and/or humor; and • refrains from monopolizing talk time. Comments:
				Critical thinking	Student contributions • are thorough and logical; • are clear and organized; • make reference to big ideas, underlying principles, and/or essential questions; and • include insightful questions or questions for clarification as needed. Comments:

3	2	1	0	Skill	Standard Peer Evaluator's Name: _____
				Evidence of preparation and comprehension	The student demonstrates • accurate comprehension of the assigned reading and discussion questions; • evidence of preparation by making reference to assigned reading; and • evidence of preparation by making no fewer than two substantive contributions. Comments:

Levels of proficiency: 3 = Above average, 2 = Average, 1 = Below average, and 0 = Not observed.

Peer Assessor to Complete for the Next Panel Discussion

Panel Discussion Rubric   **Participant's Name:** _____

3	2	1	0	Skill	Standard Peer Evaluator's Name: _____
				Oral communication	When speaking, the student • demonstrates good eye contact and assertive, engaged body language; • uses standard English (grammar/usage/word choice) appropriately; • projects voice clearly with appropriate volume, inflection, and fluency; and • conveys ideas with precision (gets to the point) and clarity (easy to follow). Comments:
				Human interaction	When listening and/or responding to others, the student • acknowledges the speaker with appropriate eye contact and engaged body language; • shows tact when engaging others in conversation, acknowledges others' contributions; • builds rapport by demonstrating supportiveness, warmth, and/or humor; and • refrains from monopolizing talk time. Comments:
				Critical thinking	Student contributions • are thorough and logical; • are clear and organized; • make reference to big ideas, underlying principles, and/or essential questions; and • include insightful questions or questions for clarification as needed. Comments:

3	2	1	0	Skill	Standard Peer Evaluator's Name: _____
				Evidence of preparation and comprehension	The student demonstrates • accurate comprehension of the assigned reading and discussion questions; • evidence of preparation by making reference to assigned reading; and • evidence of preparation by making no fewer than two substantive contributions. Comments:
Levels of proficiency: 3 = Above average, 2 = Average, 1 = Below average, and 0 = Not observed.					

EXERCISE: PANEL DISCUSSION #3

What is the most important factor that influences student learning? What is the least influential factor that influences student learning?

Student to Complete as Self-Assessment
(if a digital recording of the performance was made)

Panel Discussion Rubric   **Participant's Name:** _____

3	2	1	0	Skill	Standard Peer Evaluator's Name: _____
				Oral communication	When speaking, the student • demonstrates good eye contact and assertive, engaged body language; • uses standard English (grammar/usage/word choice) appropriately; • projects voice clearly with appropriate volume, inflection, and fluency; and • conveys ideas with precision (gets to the point) and clarity (easy to follow). Comments:
				Human interaction	When listening and/or responding to others, the student • acknowledges the speaker with appropriate eye contact and engaged body language; • shows tact when engaging others in conversation, acknowledges others' contributions; • builds rapport by demonstrating supportiveness, warmth, and/or humor; and • refrains from monopolizing talk time. Comments:
				Critical thinking	Student contributions • are thorough and logical; • are clear and organized; • make reference to big ideas, underlying principles, and/or essential questions; and • include insightful questions or questions for clarification as needed. Comments:

3	2	1	0	Skill	Standard Peer Evaluator's Name: _____
				Evidence of preparation and comprehension	The student demonstrates • accurate comprehension of the assigned reading and discussion questions; • evidence of preparation by making reference to assigned reading; and • evidence of preparation by making no fewer than two substantive contributions. Comments:
Levels of proficiency: 3 = Above average, 2 = Average, 1 = Below average, and 0 = Not observed.

Peer Assessor to Complete for the Next Panel Discussion

Panel Discussion Rubric   **Participant's Name:** _____

3	2	1	0	Skill	Standard Peer Evaluator's Name: _____
				Oral communication	When speaking, the student • demonstrates good eye contact and assertive, engaged body language; • uses standard English (grammar/usage/word choice) appropriately; • projects voice clearly with appropriate volume, inflection, and fluency; and • conveys ideas with precision (gets to the point) and clarity (easy to follow). Comments:
				Human interaction	When listening and/or responding to others, the student • acknowledges the speaker with appropriate eye contact and engaged body language; • shows tact when engaging others in conversation, acknowledges others' contributions; • builds rapport by demonstrating supportiveness, warmth, and/or humor; and • refrains from monopolizing talk time. Comments:
				Critical thinking	Student contributions • are thorough and logical; • are clear and organized; • make reference to big ideas, underlying principles, and/or essential questions; and • include insightful questions or questions for clarification as needed. Comments:

3	2	1	0	Skill	Standard Peer Evaluator's Name: _____
				Evidence of preparation and comprehension	The student demonstrates • accurate comprehension of the assigned reading and discussion questions; • evidence of preparation by making reference to assigned reading; and • evidence of preparation by making no fewer than two substantive contributions. Comments:
Levels of proficiency: 3 = Above average, 2 = Average, 1 = Below average, and 0 = Not observed.					

EXERCISE: PANEL DISCUSSION #4—HOT SEAT QUESTION

Pretend that each one of you is a seasoned classroom teacher. Your building administrator has announced that the curriculum budget has been slashed for the upcoming year. Imagine that each of you is in desperate need of curriculum money to pay for the textbooks you have already requested, but only one of you can go ahead with the purchase. Persuasively advocate for your own classroom to receive the money. [The audience will determine which panelist was the most professional persuader of all.]

**Student to Complete as Self-Assessment
(if a digital recording of the performance was made)**

Panel Discussion Rubric   **Participant's Name:** _____

3	2	1	0	Skill	Standard Peer Evaluator's Name: _____
				Oral communication	When speaking, the student • demonstrates good eye contact and assertive, engaged body language; • uses standard English (grammar/usage/word choice) appropriately; • projects voice clearly with appropriate volume, inflection, and fluency; and • conveys ideas with precision (gets to the point) and clarity (easy to follow). Comments:
				Human interaction	When listening and/or responding to others, the student • acknowledges the speaker with appropriate eye contact and engaged body language; • shows tact when engaging others in conversation, acknowledges others' contributions; • builds rapport by demonstrating supportiveness, warmth, and/or humor; and • refrains from monopolizing talk time. Comments:
				Critical thinking	Student contributions • are thorough and logical; • are clear and organized; • make reference to big ideas, underlying principles, and/or essential questions; and • include insightful questions or questions for clarification as needed. Comments:

3	2	1	0	Skill	Standard Peer Evaluator's Name: _____
				Evidence of preparation and comprehension	The student demonstrates • accurate comprehension of the assigned reading and discussion questions; • evidence of preparation by making reference to assigned reading; and • evidence of preparation by making no fewer than two substantive contributions. Comments:

Levels of proficiency: 3 = Above average, 2 = Average, 1 = Below average, and 0 = Not observed.

As you develop confidence and greater proficiency with critical thinking skills, you will increasingly adeptly raise new points (other than those raised in the assignment), challenge others' thinking, and restate others' points for the sake of clarity. As your oral communication skills and interpersonal skills develop, you will more consistently demonstrate sustained eye contact with the person speaking, show courtesy by "sharing the air" with others, and demonstrate tactful techniques for disagreeing or challenging other's positions.

📝 THINK AND WRITE

Compare the peer assessment feedback you received with your self-assessments. In which areas do you demonstrate the greatest competency? In which areas must you continue to strive and grow?

MOCK TEACHER INTERVIEWS

Numerous studies of hiring practices of K-12 schools indicate that "academic ability was considered subordinate to interpersonal skills" (Guarino, Santibanez, & Daley, 2006, p. 184). In other words, many districts place more weight upon the interpersonal skills of the candidate than their academic ability.

Presuming your transcript and resume indicate adequate academic ability for the teaching position posted, the astute district leader will scrutinize your people skills during the teacher interview to discern your dispositions and competencies that are not revealed on the resume.

WEBCONNECT

Search the web for credible websites that describe the interpersonal skills that employers are seeking. Locate at least one list of "dos" and one list of "don'ts" in this context, and prepare to share your findings with classmates.

LET'S TALK

In small groups, share highlights of the aforementioned lists of "dos" and "don'ts." What themes seemed to emerge in both categories? Compare those themes with the categories and descriptors delineated in the rubric that follows.

Mock "Teaching Position" Interview   **Interviewee's Name:** _____

3	2	1	0	Skill	Standard Interviewer's Name: _____
				Oral communication	Uses standard English appropriately and avoids "verbal fillers." Projects voice clearly with appropriate volume and inflection. Demonstrates good eye contact and engaged body language. Hand gestures are appropriate and support the speaker's message. Additional comments:
				Critical thinking	Demonstrates clarity of thought when answering questions or asking pertinent questions. Uses educational terminology appropriately. Cites personal teaching experiences with specificity to support and validate answers provided. Additional comments:
				Human interaction	Demonstrates active listening skills such as head nodding and note taking. Smiles often and conveys warmth and interest in the interviewer. Develops rapport with others. Additional comments:
				Leadership	Demonstrates alertness, self-assurance, enthusiasm, and self-direction. Initiates conversation and opportunities to articulate personal strengths and passions. Additional comments:
General comments:					

THINK AND WRITE

In which areas do you feel most prepared for the interview? Which of the rubric categories will you need to invest the most time and energy in developing? Explain.

EXERCISE—MOCK INTERVIEW: LEVEL ONE

Ask your instructor for a list of possible interview questions that local administrators are likely to ask when you interview for a teaching position. Alternate turns answering each question provided. Ask your instructor for suggestions as to the best approaches to answer questions that are most difficult for you to answer. As you complete this exercise, complete a peer assessment form for a classmate so that all students receive some preliminary feedback on their interviewing skills before participating in Level Two.

Peer-Assessment

Mock "Teaching Position" Interview   **Interviewee's Name:** _____

3	2	1	0	Skill	Standard Interviewer's Name: _____
				Oral communication	Uses standard English appropriately and avoids "verbal fillers." Projects voice clearly with appropriate volume and inflection. Demonstrates good eye contact and engaged body language. Hand gestures are appropriate and support the speaker's message. Additional comments:
				Critical thinking	Demonstrates clarity of thought when answering questions or asking pertinent questions. Uses educational terminology appropriately. Cites personal teaching experiences with specificity to support and validate answers provided. Additional comments:
				Human interaction	Demonstrates active listening skills such as head nodding and note taking. Smiles often and conveys warmth and interest in the interviewer. Develops rapport with others. Additional comments:
				Leadership	Demonstrates alertness, self-assurance, enthusiasm, and self-direction. Initiates conversation and opportunities to articulate personal strengths and passions. Additional comments:
General comments:					

EXERCISE—MOCK INTERVIEW: LEVEL TWO

In groups of three, take turns playing the following roles: interviewer, interviewee, and recorder. Conduct an interview of no more than 5–7 minutes per person, alternating the questions asked among the three interviews. Use the digital recording of each interview to prepare peer assessments or self-assessments.

Self-Assessment

Mock "Teaching Position" Interview   **Interviewee's Name:** _____

3	2	1	0	Skill	Standard Interviewer's Name: _____
				Oral communication	Uses standard English appropriately and avoids "verbal fillers." Projects voice clearly with appropriate volume and inflection. Demonstrates good eye contact and engaged body language. Hand gestures are appropriate and support the speaker's message. Additional comments:
				Critical thinking	Demonstrates clarity of thought when answering questions or asking pertinent questions. Uses educational terminology appropriately. Cites personal teaching experiences with specificity to support and validate answers provided. Additional comments:
				Human interaction	Demonstrates active listening skills such as head nodding and note taking. Smiles often and conveys warmth and interest in the interviewer. Develops rapport with others. Additional comments:
				Leadership	Demonstrates alertness, self-assurance, enthusiasm, and self-direction. Initiates conversation and opportunities to articulate personal strengths and passions. Additional comments:
				General comments:	

📝 THINK AND WRITE

Compare the peer assessment feedback you received with your self-assessments. In which areas do you demonstrate the greatest competency? In which areas must you continue to strive and grow?

INTERVIEW FOLLOW-UP

It is a professional courtesy to write a thank-you within 24 hours of being interviewed. There once was a day when all thank-yous were to be handwritten. However, it is now acceptable to e-mail thank-yous. Take note, though, that texting thank-yous is not yet deemed professional.

LITERACY SKILLS

7

CHAPTER

Continuous improvement is better than delayed perfection.

Mark Twain

The learner will:

- practice and refine writing skills on education-related topics;
- compose an educator's resume;
- practice and refine oral reading fluency; and
- reflect upon self-assessment and peer assessment of practice performances.

Effective teachers demonstrate strong literacy skills. Let us begin with writing proficiency. Compose essays for each of the following, making certain to comply with the Writing Rubric that follows the list of prompts.

WRITING PROMPTS

In your vision of teaching, what are the most important things teachers do for their students? Explain.

What personal passions do you think will enhance your teaching? Explain.

Describe a role model or mentor who epitomizes the traits of an effective teacher. Explain how this person has influenced you.

Describe those field experiences that have heightened your awareness of the advantages and disadvantages of teaching. How has this awareness impacted your desire to become a teacher?

Writing Sample Rubric

Competency	Focus/Content	Organization	Style, Grammar, and Usage	Spelling, Punctuation, and Legibility
Above average **4**	Addresses all points of the prompt provided Convincingly develops a substantive single focus and purpose related to the prompt Paragraphs are fully developed with topic sentences related to the prompt	Evinces a tight organizational structure appropriate to the audience and purpose Paragraphs are logically ordered Transitions between paragraphs are clear and cohesive Introduction engages audience and addresses purpose Conclusion provides clinching statement or appropriate closing	Words are precisely chosen Sentences are clear, coherent, and varied in length and structure as appropriate Grammar and usage consistently conform to the conventions of Standard Edited American English	Spelling and punctuation consistently conform to the conventions of Standard Edited American English Size and formation of letters consistently make the selection easy to read
Average **3**	Addresses the central points of the prompt provided Develops a substantive single focus and purpose related to the prompt Most paragraphs are fairly well developed with topic sentences	Organization is appropriate to the purpose Paragraphs are logically linked via topic sentences Transitions between paragraphs are usually clear and cohesive Begins with an introduction that addresses purpose and ends with a clear conclusion	Most sentences are clear, coherent, and varied in style and structure Word choice adequately conveys the message Free of serious errors in grammar and usage	Free of serious errors in spelling and punctuation Most letters are properly sized and formed to make the selection easy to read
Below average **2**	Addresses some points of the prompt provided May develop a substantive focus and purpose; however, it does not directly address the prompt May occasionally wander from central idea(s) related to the prompt Paragraphs may lack topic sentences related to the prompt or may lack substantive support	The overall organization is easy to follow, but may be inappropriate for the audience or purpose Paragraphs may be mis-sequenced Transitions between paragraphs may be ineffective Introduction and conclusion evident but ineffective	Sentences are generally clear and correct; however, some may be basic, choppy, or lack variety Word choice lacks precision and minimizes the writer's credibility Errors in grammar and usage occasionally interfere with communication and minimize writer's credibility	Errors in spelling and/or punctuation occasionally interfere with communication and minimize writer's credibility Letters are generally properly sized and formed; however, deficiencies in either trait occasionally interfere with reading
Poor **1**	Fails to address the prompt provided Paragraphs are poorly constructed with limited support	Organization structure is illogical, unclear, or inappropriate Paragraphs frequently seem unrelated or repetitive Introduction and conclusion are missing or weak	Sentences are frequently basic, choppy, or repetitive in structure and may lack clarity Inappropriate or inaccurate word use detracts from message Multiple errors in grammar and usage impede communication and undermine the writer's credibility	Multiple errors in spelling and/or punctuation impede communication and undermine the writer's credibility Sizing and/or formation of letters consistently impedes reading

Adapted from Spring Arbor University

WEBCONNECT

Search the Internet to find well-written examples of each of the following:

- Introduction letters
- Field-trip permission forms
- Invitation to open houses
- Educator resume (See "Appendix" for sample resumes and other excellent support resources for the development of cover letters, resumes, and even interview preparation.)

EXERCISE

Draft your own personal version of each of the aforementioned types of educator correspondence.

LET'S TALK

Share your writing pieces with one another. Be certain to use sandwich language when delivering feedback.

EXERCISE

Locate a teacher's manual for one of the grade-level content areas you will teach. Rehearse reading portions aloud paying close attention to the reading fluency rubric that follows.

Reading FLUENCY Assessment: Multidimensional Fluency Scale

	4	3	2	1
Phrasing	Generally well phrased, mostly in clause and sentence units; smooth transitions between sentences	Mixture of run-ons, mid-sentence pauses for breath, and possibly some choppiness; reasonable stress and intonation	Frequent two- and three-word phrases giving the impression of choppy reading; improper stress and intonation that fails to make the end of sentences and clauses	Monotonic, with little sense of phrase boundaries; frequent word by word reading
Smoothness	Generally smooth reading with some breaks, but word structure difficulties are resolved quickly, usually through self-correction	Occasional breaks in smoothness caused by difficulties with specific words and/or structures	Several tough spots in text, where extended pauses, hesitations, etc. are more frequent and disruptive	Frequent extended pauses, hesitations, false starts, sound outs, repetitions, and/or multiple attempts
Pace	Consistently conversational	Uneven mixture of fast and slow	Moderately slow	Slow and laborious
Intonation	Reads with appropriate intonation throughout the story; expression indicates understanding of nuances	Mostly appropriate intonation and expressive at key points in the story	Occasional instances of appropriate intonation; responds to bold print by reading louder	Read with monotone and/or little expressive evidence of understanding nuances

Adapted from Zufel and Rasinski (1989)

⧉ EXERCISE #1

Read aloud for 3 minutes or less as one peer evaluates your oral reading fluency and another digitally records you doing so.

Peer Assessment

Reading FLUENCY Assessment: Multidimensional Fluency Scale

	4	3	2	1
Phrasing	Generally well phrased, mostly in clause and sentence units; smooth transitions between sentences	Mixture of run-ons, mid-sentence pauses for breath, and possibly some choppiness; reasonable stress and intonation	Frequent two- and three-word phrases giving the impression of choppy reading; improper stress and intonation that fails to make the end of sentences and clauses	Monotonic, with little sense of phrase boundaries; frequent word by word reading
Smoothness	Generally smooth reading with some breaks, but word structure difficulties are resolved quickly, usually through self-correction	Occasional breaks in smoothness caused by difficulties with specific words and/or structures	Several tough spots in text, where extended pauses, hesitations, etc. are more frequent and disruptive	Frequent extended pauses, hesitations, false starts, sound outs, repetitions, and/or multiple attempts
Pace	Consistently conversational	Uneven mixture of fast and slow	Moderately slow	Slow and laborious
Intonation	Reads with appropriate intonation throughout the story; expression indicates understanding of nuances	Mostly appropriate intonation and expressive at key points in the story	Occasional instances of appropriate intonation; responds to bold print by reading louder	Read with monotone and/or little expressive evidence of understanding nuances

Adapted from Zufel and Rasinski (1989)

Self-Assessment

Reading FLUENCY Assessment: Multidimensional Fluency Scale

	4	3	2	1
Phrasing	Generally well phrased, mostly in clause and sentence units; smooth transitions between sentences	Mixture of run-ons, mid-sentence pauses for breath, and possibly some choppiness; reasonable stress and intonation	Frequent two- and three-word phrases giving the impression of choppy reading; improper stress and intonation that fails to make the end of sentences and clauses	Monotonic, with little sense of phrase boundaries; frequent word by word reading
Smoothness	Generally smooth reading with some breaks, but word structure difficulties are resolved quickly, usually through self-correction	Occasional breaks in smoothness caused by difficulties with specific words and/or structures	Several tough spots in text, where extended pauses, hesitations, etc. are more frequent and disruptive	Frequent extended pauses, hesitations, false starts, sound outs, repetitions, and/or multiple attempts

	4	3	2	1
Pace	Consistently conversational	Uneven mixture of fast and slow	Moderately slow	Slow and laborious
Intonation	Reads with appropriate intonation throughout the story; expression indicates understanding of nuances	Mostly appropriate intonation and expressive at key points in the story	Occasional instances of appropriate intonation; responds to bold print by reading louder	Read with monotone and/or little expressive evidence of understanding nuances

Adapted from Zufel and Rasinski (1989)

 ## EXERCISE #2

Read aloud for 3 minutes or less as one peer evaluates your oral reading fluency and other digitally records you doing so.

Peer Assessment

Reading FLUENCY Assessment: Multidimensional Fluency Scale

	4	3	2	1
Phrasing	Generally well phrased, mostly in clause and sentence units; smooth transitions between sentences	Mixture of run-ons, mid-sentence pauses for breath, and possibly some choppiness; reasonable stress and intonation	Frequent two- and three-word phrases giving the impression of choppy reading; improper stress and intonation that fails to make the end of sentences and clauses	Monotonic, with little sense of phrase boundaries; frequent word by word reading
Smoothness	Generally smooth reading with some breaks, but word structure difficulties are resolved quickly, usually through self-correction	Occasional breaks in smoothness caused by difficulties with specific words and/or structures	Several tough spots in text, where extended pauses, hesitations, etc. are more frequent and disruptive	Frequent extended pauses, hesitations, false starts, sound outs, repetitions, and/or multiple attempts
Pace	Consistently conversational	Uneven mixture of fast and slow	Moderately slow	Slow and laborious
Intonation	Reads with appropriate intonation throughout the story; expression indicates understanding of nuances	Mostly appropriate intonation and expressive at key points in the story	Occasional instances of appropriate intonation; responds to bold print by reading louder	Read with monotone and/or little expressive evidence of understanding nuances

Adapted from Zufel and Rasinski (1989)

Self-Assessment

Reading FLUENCY Assessment: Multidimensional Fluency Scale

	4	3	2	1
Phrasing	Generally well phrased, mostly in clause and sentence units; smooth transitions between sentences	Mixture of run-ons, mid-sentence pauses for breath, and possibly some choppiness; reasonable stress and intonation	Frequent two- and three-word phrases giving the impression of choppy reading; improper stress and intonation that fails to make the end of sentences and clauses	Monotonic, with little sense of phrase boundaries; frequent word by word reading
Smoothness	Generally smooth reading with some breaks, but word structure difficulties are resolved quickly, usually through self-correction	Occasional breaks in smoothness caused by difficulties with specific words and/or structures	Several tough spots in text, where extended pauses, hesitations, etc. are more frequent and disruptive	Frequent extended pauses, hesitations, false starts, sound outs, repetitions, and/or multiple attempts
Pace	Consistently conversational	Uneven mixture of fast and slow	Moderately slow	Slow and laborious
Intonation	Reads with appropriate intonation throughout the story; expression indicates understanding of nuances	Mostly appropriate intonation and expressive at key points in the story	Occasional instances of appropriate intonation; responds to bold print by reading louder	Read with monotone and/or little expressive evidence of understanding nuances

Adapted from Zufel and Rasinski (1989)

 EXERCISE #3

Read aloud for 3 minutes or less as one peer evaluates your oral reading fluency and other digitally records you doing so.

Peer Assessment

Reading FLUENCY Assessment: Multidimensional Fluency Scale

	4	3	2	1
Phrasing	Generally well phrased, mostly in clause and sentence units; smooth transitions between sentences	Mixture of run-ons, mid-sentence pauses for breath, and possibly some choppiness; reasonable stress and intonation	Frequent two- and three-word phrases giving the impression of choppy reading; improper stress and intonation that fails to make the end of sentences and clauses	Monotonic, with little sense of phrase boundaries; frequent word by word reading
Smoothness	Generally smooth reading with some breaks, but word structure difficulties are resolved quickly, usually through self-correction	Occasional breaks in smoothness caused by difficulties with specific words and/or structures	Several tough spots in text, where extended pauses, hesitations, etc. are more frequent and disruptive	Frequent extended pauses, hesitations, false starts, sound outs, repetitions, and/or multiple attempts

	4	3	2	1
Pace	Consistently conversational	Uneven mixture of fast and slow	Moderately slow	Slow and laborious
Intonation	Reads with appropriate intonation throughout the story; expression indicates understanding of nuances	Mostly appropriate intonation and expressive at key points in the story	Occasional instances of appropriate intonation; responds to bold print by reading louder	Read with monotone and/or little expressive evidence of understanding nuances

Self-Assessment

Reading FLUENCY Assessment: Multidimensional Fluency Scale

	4	3	2	1
Phrasing	Generally well phrased, mostly in clause and sentence units; smooth transitions between sentences	Mixture of run-ons, mid-sentence pauses for breath, and possibly some choppiness; reasonable stress and intonation	Frequent two- and three-word phrases giving the impression of choppy reading; improper stress and intonation that fails to make the end of sentences and clauses	Monotonic, with little sense of phrase boundaries; frequent word by word reading
Smoothness	Generally smooth reading with some breaks, but word structure difficulties are resolved quickly, usually through self-correction	Occasional breaks in smoothness caused by difficulties with specific words and/or structures	Several tough spots in text, where extended pauses, hesitations, etc. are more frequent and disruptive	Frequent extended pauses, hesitations, false starts, sound outs, repetitions, and/or multiple attempts
Pace	Consistently conversational	Uneven mixture of fast and slow	Moderately slow	Slow and laborious
Intonation	Reads with appropriate intonation throughout the story; expression indicates understanding of nuances	Mostly appropriate intonation and expressive at key points in the story	Occasional instances of appropriate intonation; responds to bold print by reading louder	Read with monotone and/or little expressive evidence of understanding nuances

Adapted from Zufel and Rasinski (1989)

📝 THINK AND WRITE

Compare your peer assessments and self-assessments of the previous three exercises. What are your greatest strengths? What must you do to improve?

PROFESSIONAL KNOWLEDGE

8

The only person who is educated is the one who has learned how to learn . . . and change.

Carl Rogers

In the United States, each individual state has authority to grant licensure (the right to provide services) to professionals in various fields such as education, medicine, law, and health services. Requirements for teacher licensure vary from state. For educators who aspire to teach in state-funded schools, it is imperative that those teachers are licensed to do so. Because licensure standards vary from state to state, this lesson will guide preservice teachers to locate the licensure requirements for the state in which they are being prepared.

In addition, this lesson will prompt the preservice teacher to develop a solid understanding of the teacher preparation process in his or her teacher preparation program. By developing a program completion plan and examining program expectations from the very start, preservice teachers will be best prepared to complete the program successfully and in a timely manner.

OBJECTIVES

The learner will:

- locate state-mandated teacher certification/licensure requirements;
- develop familiarity with his or her teacher preparation program's conceptual framework and program-related resources;
- ascertain program completion requirements at his or her institution; and
- compose a School of Education (SOE)-approved program completion plan.

Licensure Requirements by State

Though there is much commonality among licensure standards for teachers, each state seems to have slightly different standards than the other. For example, some states require teacher candidates to pass a nationally administered licensure test, and other states may require successful completion of a state-specific licensure test.

WEBCONNECT

Search your state's Department of Education website to locate the requirements for initial teacher licensure in your state.

 ## LET'S TALK

With a partner, discuss the requirements for initial teacher licensure you located on your state's website. Which of the requirements make sense to you? Which words or phrases are unfamiliar to you?

 ## EXERCISE

Draft a document (one page or less) formatted as a checklist of requirements for initial licensure in the state in which you are preparing to become a teacher. Use your own words to describe and explain each requirement that is not easily discernible by a lay person. Be creative with the design of your checklist.

Example:

> Requirement #1: Pass the MTTC content area test
>
> > Explanation: MTTC stands for Michigan Teacher Test for Certification. This standardized test evaluates a candidate's knowledge of the major he or she studied in college.

Your Local Program's Conceptual Framework and Requirements

A Conceptual Framework is an organized, concise articulation of a teacher preparation program's mission, values, and ideals. In many instances, it is a succinct expression of the knowledge, skills, and dispositions of the "ideal teacher" who completes the program. The Conceptual Framework is often graphically represented with words embedded within the design.

 ## WEBCONNECT

Conduct a Google search using the following words: EPP and Conceptual Framework. Be certain to search for your program's Conceptual Framework as well.

 ## LET'S TALK

With a partner, compare notes regarding the knowledge, skills, and dispositions that many teacher preparation programs have in common.

📝 **THINK AND WRITE**

Briefly summarize the knowledge, skills, and dispositions that comprise your SOE's Conceptual Framework.

📝 **THINK AND WRITE**

Which of the aforementioned knowledge, skills, and dispositions are already strengths of yours? Which areas will require the most growth and development over the course of the program? Explain.

WEBCONNECT

Locate your SOE's Handbook for Students (or an equivalent resource) that contains the policies and requirements for teacher education students within the program.

EXERCISE: Your Education Program's Policies and Procedures

Instructor/student choice: After carefully reviewing your SOE's Handbook for Students (or equivalent resource), compose one of the following based upon its contents:

Option A: an "open book" test (or two shorter quizzes).
Option B: a PowerPoint summarizing "The Road to Admission."
Option C: an informative trifold pamphlet that highlights critical policies and procedures.
Option D: a scavenger hunt of critical policies to be located in the SOE Handbook.

LET'S TALK

In small groups, share the quizzes, PowerPoints, pamphlets, and scavenger hunts created in the previous exercise. Use sandwich language to give one another feedback.

THINK AND WRITE

Delineate five "takeaways" from the aforementioned sharing exercise that you consider to be the most valuable pieces of information you will need to know to successfully complete your teacher preparation program.

EXERCISE: Develop a Resource Notebook

Begin compiling a resource notebook (hard copy or electronic) that becomes your personalized resource for navigating your teacher preparation program experience. Following are categories of information that you are strongly encouraged to gather and then file into your notebook:

1. Advisor's name, contact information, and office hours.
2. Certifiable majors/minors for elementary certification.
3. Certifiable majors/minors for secondary certification.
4. GPA requirements for the entire program.
5. Minimum grade requirement for individual courses.
6. Field experience hours: number of hours to be completed, timeline for completion, documentation requirements for field experiences.
7. Admission process and requirements.
8. Program completion plan.
9. Portfolio (or equivalency) requirements.

EXERCISE: Program Completion Plan

Draft a document of all of the required courses and practicum experiences you will need to successfully complete to be nominated for teacher licensure by your teacher education program. Order those requirements in accordance with the recommended guidelines in the Academic Catalog published by your institution.

Submit a draft of your proposed "Program Completion Plan" to your academic advisor and request constructive feedback.

LET'S TALK

With a partner, compare individualized Program Completion Plans. What accounts for the differences in course ordering and time of completion? What did you learn from reviewing one another's plans?

▦ THINK AND WRITE

What is the relationship between teacher licensure requirements in your state and the teacher preparation program requirements you must meet?

▦ THINK AND WRITE

What was the most valuable information you gleaned from this lesson? In which areas are you most in need of additional explanation and assistance?

CURRICULUM

The nicest thing about standards is that there are so many of them to choose from.

Andres S. Tanenbaum

Reduced to its essential elements, curriculum can be defined as "that which is to be taught in various content areas at various grade levels." All departments of education within each state in the United States mandate a specific set of academic expectations or standards. These academic expectations—coupled with resources, lesson plans, assessments—become a school's curriculum. The purpose of this lesson is to introduce the preservice teacher to state-mandated curriculum along with the differing codification systems for each content area.

OBJECTIVES

The learner will:

- locate K-12 curricular standards for his or her home state of licensure/certification;
- examine the prevalence of Common Core standards and Next Generation standards among states' mandated curricula;
- develop familiarity with the codification systems and organization of Common Core standards, Next Generation standards, and other state-mandated content area standards; and
- practice locating curricular standards within various documents and codification systems (Common Core, Next Generation, state-specific content areas).

In order for teachers to have a guide of what to teach, they must be able to locate their state's mandated curricular standards for each content area. Below is a chart that provides Michigan teachers with links to documents containing curricular standards by content area (English language arts, mathematics, etc.).

Sample:

Michigan Curricular Standards by Content Area				
English language arts	**Mathematics**	**Science**	**Social studies**	**Noncore content areas** (*music/arts, health/ PE, world language, technology*)
Common Core State Standards (CCSS) http://www .corestandards .org/the-standards (K-12)	Common Core State Standards (CCSS) http://www .corestandards .org/the-standards (K-12)	Next Generation Science Standards (NGSS) http://www .nextgenscience .org/next-generation-science-standards (K-12) and https://www .michigan.gov/ science (old standards K-7 and 8-High school)	Grade Level Content Expectations (GLCEs) K-8 High School Content Expectations (HSCEs) https://www .michigan .gov/ socialstudies	Michigan Merit Curriculum (visual and performing arts http://www.michigan .gov/documents/ mde/Complete_ VPAA_Expectations_ June_2011_356110_7 .pdf?20130829080837) Physical Education GLCEs and MMC (http://www .michigan.gov/ mde/0,4615,7-140-28753_64839_38684_ 29234-162275--,00 .html and http://www .michigan.gov/documents/ mde/NewMMCPE9-5-2007_ 213954_7.pdf) World Languages Standards (K-12) (http://www. michigan.gov/documents/ mde/WLSB_206824_7. pdf?20130829081320) Michigan Educational Technology Standards (METS) (PK-12) (http:// techplan.edzone.net/METS/ METS2009.pdf)

Content expectations for ECE (three- and four-year-olds) - search the http://www.michigan.gov/ website for related curricular documents.

⚙ WEBCONNECT

Search the web to determine (1) how many states have adopted Common Core State Standards (CCSS) for English language arts and mathematics and (2) if your state has adopted those CCSS.

WEBCONNECT

Search the web to determine (1) how many states have adopted Next Generation Science Standards (NGSS) and (2) if your state has adopted those NGSS.

 LET'S TALK

With a partner, answer the following questions:

Which of the state standards referenced in the Michigan chart above are "uniquely" Michigan's curricular standards? (neither Common Core nor Next Generation Science Standards)

How did you reach that conclusion? Explain.

 LET'S TALK

What are the advantages of having a common national curriculum? What are the disadvantages of having a common national curriculum?

THINK AND WRITE

If you had the authority to make the determination, would you support or reject a common national curriculum in the United States? Explain.

🌐 WEBCONNECT

Locate your state's mandated curricular standards for each of the content areas listed in the chart below.

≣ EXERCISE: State Curriculum Chart

Compose a "Curricular Standards by Content Area" chart for the state in which you will certify. (If you are certifying in the state of Michigan, select another state for this exercise.) Use the template below to complete this exercise. (*Note:* Most states provide this information via their Department of Education website.)

[insert state name] Curricular Standards by Content Area				
English language arts	Mathematics	Science	Social studies	Noncore content areas (*music/arts, health/PE, world language, technology*)

✍ THINK AND WRITE

Having completed the aforementioned exercise, share what you find to be (1) most valuable, (2) most surprising, and (3) most challenging.

CODIFICATION SYSTEMS AND ORGANIZATION

It is vital for the preservice teacher to become comfortable with the organization, codes, language, and content for each set of curricular standards. One way to do this is to utilize the concept of a scavenger hunt that leads the user through the most important parts of the physical document.

🗐 EXERCISE: SCAVENGER HUNT—PART ONE

Directions: For this exercise, we will begin with only one of the academic standards documents from above to investigate: mathematics/CCSS. Download the most current document (which is currently 93 pages long).

On what page(s) do the authors explain how to read the grade level standards? _____

Each grade level contains an "Overview" page. On this page, the domains and clusters are listed while also focusing on the consistent "Mathematical Practices." Select one grade level. List the domains for that particular grade level along with 1–4 of the related clusters for each domain.

Domain	Cluster

On the same overview page, also note the "Mathematical Practices." List 1–3 of the Mathematical Practices that you feel you can see yourself implementing well in your lessons to teach these clusters and standards. For more information about the practices, see pages 6–8.

1. _____

2. _____

3. _____

Within each cluster and domain are *content expectations*. For ease in referencing expectations, each expectation has been coded. However, the coding system for content expectations within each content area (mathematics, English language arts) is slightly different. *Be certain to review the coding system for each content area before* attempting to decipher the meaning of each letter and number in the code.

For example, Common Core content expectations are coded in the following order:

- grade level
- domain
- content expectation number

Note: The clusters are not part of the code.

Let's practice. If you encounter a Common Core code of "2.OA.3," you can immediately infer the following:

2 = second grade

OA = Operations and Algebraic Thinking

3 = content expectation number

The aforementioned code references the following grade level content expectation:

Determine whether a group of objects (up to 20) has an odd or even number of members, for example, by pairing objects or counting them by 2s; write an equation to express an even number as a sum of two equal addends.

Now, it's your turn. Find the CCSS coded: 6.SP.4.

What is the grade? _____

What is the domain? _____

Write the full Common Core State Standard below:

_____

_____

_____

_____

LET'S TALK

Having completed the aforementioned exercise, share what you find to be (1) most valuable, (2) most surprising, and (3) most challenging.

EXERCISE: SCAVENGER HUNT—Part TWO

Directions: With a partner, examine the codification system and organization of any *one* of the content areas identified in your state-specific Curricular Standards chart. Draft a scavenger hunter for your classmates to complete.

Compose the scavenger hunt below, making certain to guide the "hunter" through the codification of content expectations.

SCAVENGER HUNT

EXERCISE: SCAVENGER HUNT—Part THREE

Directions: Exchange copies of the newly created scavenger hunts. Complete as many of these peer-created scavenger hunts as your instructor indicates.

LET'S TALK

Having completed the aforementioned exercise, share what you found to be (1) most valuable, (2) most surprising, and (3) most challenging.

THINK AND WRITE

Compose a "Top 5" list of the most valuable insights you gleaned from this section of Chapter 8.

Knowing the academic expectations (whether they are the CCSS, NGSS, or other state-mandated expectations) that a teacher is responsible for teaching and assessing is just the beginning of the lesson planning process. Teachers must next consider the level of taxonomy of each expectation, how long that expectation will take to teach and to what depth, and what other resources will be needed to effectively reach each student. Some teachers collaborate to create supporting documents such as curriculum maps or scope and sequence charts. These supporting documents get teachers one step closer to an organized, intentionally sequential, and meaningful learning environment.

LESSON PLANNING

He who fails to plan is planning to fail.

Winston Churchill

Effective teachers are proficient planners. Not only do they plan the flow of activities and student movement throughout the day, they carefully design and execute lesson plans (LPs) composed of critical elements that set students up for success. What are those "must have" elements of an effective LP? How does a preservice teacher even begin to compose properly ordered LPs with these vital elements? This section of Chapter 8 offers the preservice teacher a "crash course" in Lesson Planning 101.

OBJECTIVES

- Identify and define each of the critical elements of an effective LP;
- Locate verbs described as "Key Words" in Bloom's taxonomy and use those verbs when composing standards-based objectives; and
- Compose one mini-LP using the backward design method.

CRITICAL ELEMENTS OF AN EFFECTIVE LP

Teachers write a variety of LPs for varying purposes. Though approaches to teaching may range from direct instruction to inquiry and discovery, the effective teacher always keeps in mind that there are critical elements of direct instruction that scaffold student learning at its best.

EXERCISE

Read the chart below aloud with a partner. As you finish reading each element and related description, develop a gesture or body movement that will help you remember the name of the critical element described.

Critical Elements of an Effective LP	
Elements of Lesson Plans	**Descriptions of Elements**
Identify the curricular standard	This is a series of letters and/or numbers linked to Common Core standards, Next Generation standards, or another state/district-mandated standard curriculum standard.
Objective	This is a statement of what the learner will know or be able to do by the end of the lesson.
	Reduce the objective down to a measurable statement that begins with "The learner will . . ." followed by a verb chosen from Bloom's taxonomy.
Anticipatory set	This is how you, as a teacher, capture the attention of your students. Do so by connecting the current lesson with prior experiences or previous lessons.
	Some educators call this element the "hook," as though you are reeling in fish.
	Example: "Class, do you remember when we visited the planetarium last month and saw a grouping of stars called the Big Dipper? Today, we will be examining one of the largest stars within that . . ."
State purpose and objective	This is what you, as a teacher, tell your learners the objective and reason for the lesson in "student-friendly language."
	Remember to include both parts: the statement of what learners will accomplish through this lesson, and why it is important for them to do so.
Input	This is a description of what you and/or your students will be doing during this lesson to acquire the new material or skills.
	Example: The teacher may read a selection to the class or teach a new concept, students may watch a short video clip, students may read a section in the textbook with a partner, etc.
Modeling	This is how you, as a teacher, show students how to do something. It is very helpful when you "think out loud" while doing so.
	Example: While teaching a math concept by doing a story problem on the board, think aloud: "Three more than 2x . . ." let's see, "more" means addition . . . "2x" means I need to multiply . . .)

Guided practice	After watching you (as a teacher) model a skill, students will then attempt to perform the skill with the support and/or assistance of a partner. While students attempt this skill semi-independently, you will walk around the classroom to assist as needed.
	Example: Each student will attempt to complete a story problem with the help of a partner.
	*An alternative approach is to have each student attempt the story problem and write his or her answer on a personal whiteboard. You, as a teacher, will then ask the students to hold up their whiteboards to show you their answers. This gives you an indication of whether or not students are able to move on to independent practice or if they needed additional guided practice.
Closure	At the conclusion of the lesson, you (as a teacher) ask students to share what they learned—related to the LP objective.
	Example: A "quick write" at the end of class, choral responses of key points learned, a "ticket out the door" where students must hand the quick write to you before they exit the room, etc.
Independent practice	Once students have demonstrated that they can successfully complete the prescribed task with limited assistance from a partner or the teacher, the student is then assigned independent seat work or homework to practice independently.
Assessment	This is the teacher's plan for "checking for understanding" throughout the lesson as well as at the conclusion of the lesson (a quiz, a paper, or some form of homework).
Differentiation considerations	These are modifications that may be used to reach learners at a variety of different instructional levels.
Reflection	As a teacher, ask yourself, "How and to what extent did the learners achieve the LP objective(s)? What could I have done differently to increase student learning and student engagement?"

 LET'S TALK

Exchange answers to the following questions with a partner: Which of the LP elements are most closely related to others? Which elements are most difficult to match with their respective descriptions?

🗐 EXERCISE: Match Names of LP Elements with Descriptions

Remove this page from the workbook (or print a copy of the chart from your e-book) and cut the chart above along the lines so that each LP element is separated from its corresponding description. Shuffle the slips of paper, then attempt to recreate the chart by matching the LP element with its corresponding description.

🗐 EXERCISE: QUIZ—ELEMENTS OF AN EFFECTIVE LESSON PLAN

Match the following lesson plan element names with the most closely related description listed below:

a. Curriculum standard
b. Objective
c. Anticipatory set
d. Purpose
e. Input
f. Modeling
g. Guided practice
h. Independent practice
i. Assessment
j. Closure
k. Differentiation considerations

1. This is a series of letters and numbers from the state-mandated curriculum.
2. This is a description of what you and/or your students will be doing during this lesson to acquire the new material or skills.
3. For this element, students tell you what they learned—related to the objective—before you dismiss them from class.
4. This is an activity the student will complete *with* teacher guidance or peer assistance so that the teacher can discern whether or not he or she may assign independent practice.
5. This element grabs the students' attention and introduces the lesson.
6. This element includes several possible modifications that can be made to reach learners who are functioning at a variety of instructional levels.
7. The student will complete this activity to demonstrate proficiency *without* teacher guidance or peer assistance.
8. This element is composed of teacher-led examples and teacher "think alouds" or demonstrations of competencies associated with the lesson.
9. This element is often just a portion of a state-mandated standard. It is written at the top of the lesson plan, and begins with the phrase "The learner will . . ."
10. This element is a clear statement to students from the teacher—expressing an explanation of what learners will know and be able to do as a result of the lesson, and why it is important for them to do so.
11. This element is composed of both formal and informal evaluations of student performance that the teacher uses to determine if learners have met the prescribed objectives.

WEBCONNECT: LESSON PLAN TEMPLATES

Locate your School of Education's LP template(s). If none are available, search the web for LP templates that most align with your instructor's description of "best practice" when designing LP. Download those templates to be used as guides when writing future lesson plans.

LET'S TALK

In small groups, have each person share at least two of the LP templates that he or she chose to download. After everyone has shared, identify the commonalities among the templates.

LET'S TALK

In small groups, develop consensus around responses to each of the following questions: How and to what extent do LP templates differ by content area and grade level? If only 6 of the 12 critical elements could be used—and the others were to be deemed "optional"—which six would you choose? Explain.

BLOOM'S TAXONOMY

WEBCONNECT: BLOOM'S TAXONOMY

Locate the verbs (identified as "Key Words") used at each level of Bloom's taxonomy of cognitive learning domains. Do the same for Bloom's *revised* taxonomy of cognitive learning domains. Save lists of these verbs to be used when writing objectives for the lesson planning exercise that follows.

LET'S TALK

In small groups, discuss responses to the following questions: What is a taxonomy? Of what practical value to teachers is a "taxonomy of learning domains"? In your experience, are the higher-level domains (creating, evaluating, etc.) more difficult than the lower domains (remembering, explaining, etc.)? In your opinion, are the lower-level domains less important than the higher-level domains? Explain.

THINK AND WRITE

Write out a synopsis of your personal answers to the aforementioned "Let's Talk" questions.

"BACKWARD DESIGN" LESSON PLANNING

Without a doubt, effective teachers begin the lesson planning process with the end in mind. The following four steps will guide you to compose an LP in the proper order:

FOUR-STEP "BACKWARD DESIGN"

Step 1: Locate the curricular standard to be addressed.

a. Select only a *portion* of the standard that can be adequately addressed in an LP of the specified length of time.
b. Check out teacher resources (a teacher's manual, a teacher's edition of a textbook, or a local school's curriculum guide) for samples of grade-level-appropriate objectives based upon the standard you selected.

Step 2: Compose the LP objective.

a. Begin with "The learner will . . ."
b. Choose the most appropriate, *measurable*, Bloom's taxonomy verb to guide student accomplishment.

Step 3: Design the assessment.

a. What will every learner be able to do to demonstrate that they have accomplished the objective?
b. What evidence will be generated to prove that *all* learners have accomplished that objective?

c. Don't fall into the "trap" of assessing only a few learners.

d. How will you evaluate the performance of each individual?

e. Ask yourself, "Does this assessment match my objective perfectly?" If not, alter it until it does. This is the most common error in LP design.

Step 4: Write the remainder of your LP.

a. Follow the LP template provided by your School of Education or course instructor.

b. Carefully read the descriptions of each element of instructional procedure so that the elements you develop for your LP comply with the guidelines.

c. Type your LP into the template provided by your school or instructor.

EXERCISE: COMPOSE A LESSON PLAN

With a partner, compose an LP for a content area of your choice within your desired area of teacher certification/licensure. Follow the four-step backward design strategy when doing so.

THINK AND WRITE

What was the most challenging aspect of designing the LP? What was the easiest aspect of designing this LP? Explain your answers to both questions.

LET'S TALK

Exchange the LP you and your partner composed with another pair in your classroom. Using sandwich language, give one another feedback on the quality of the LP design. Be certain to examine how and to what extent the LP assessment matches the curricular standard and stated objective.

THINK AND WRITE

What was the most valuable feedback that you and your partner received on the LP you developed together? Which critical element of LPs is the most difficult for you to grasp or compose at this time? Explain.

ASSESSMENT, MANAGEMENT, AND ORGANIZATION

The important question is not how assessment is defined but whether assessment information is used.

Palomba and Banta

In the context of the field of education, assessment can be defined as "a measurement of student performance or learning." Management and organization are often mentioned as a pair, and that pairing in an educational context refers to how an educator shapes student behavior, maintains order within the classroom, and handles time and materials.

At some point in your professional development as an educator, you will likely enroll in semester-long courses on the subjects of assessment and classroom management. With that in mind, this section of Chapter 8 was designed to provide only the most basic tenets of both. To the learner entering an educator preparation program, this lesson provides a brief introduction to the topics. To the preservice teacher preparing for more intensive field experiences or student teaching, this section provides a refresher of previous course work on these subjects.

OBJECTIVES

The learner will:

- develop an understanding of the terms *assessment* and *classroom management* and *organization* as they are used in the field of education;
- explain how assessment is an integral component of the instructional process;
- explain the roles that formative assessment and summative assessment play in an educator's instructional practices; and
- interview classroom teachers to glean insights regarding best practices relative to classroom management, organization of the learning environment, and assessment practices.

ASSESSMENT

Effective educators are continuously assessing student performance and learning. Assessment that is done for the purpose of informing the teacher's instruction is deemed formative assessment, and assessments conducted for the purpose of final evaluations are deemed summative assessment.

Carefully read and contemplate the information provided in the assessment diagram that follows:

The Role of FORMATIVE and SUMMATIVE Assessments

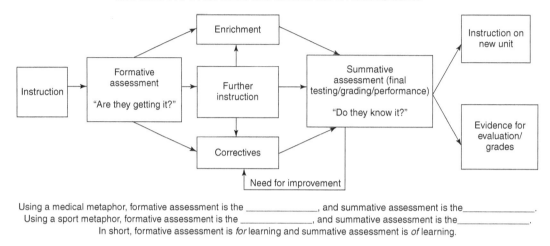

Using a medical metaphor, formative assessment is the _____, and summative assessment is the_____.
Using a sport metaphor, formative assessment is the _____, and summative assessment is the_____.
In short, formative assessment is *for* learning and summative assessment is *of* learning.

What **we do with the results** determines whether an assessment is formative or summative.

 ## LET'S TALK

In small groups, derive consensus responses to the metaphors and fill in the blanks presented at the bottom of the chart. Then, compose a third metaphor to share with the class.

THINK AND WRITE

Explain the roles that formative assessment and summative assessment play in an educator's instructional practices.

LET'S TALK

With a partner, develop a response to the following question: "Are quizzes inherently formative assessments or summative assessments?" Be certain to make reference to the content in the assessment diagram to support your answer.

📝 THINK AND WRITE

Explain how assessment is an integral component of the instructional process.

MANAGEMENT AND ORGANIZATION

Numerous research studies report that classroom management is among the most difficult skills to master as a new teacher. Freiberg (2002) also asserts that organization is one of the most difficult skills for new teacher to acquire. Perhaps classroom management is a form of tacit knowledge that is difficult to express, and—therefore—extremely difficult to teach in a university classroom setting. Nonetheless, both management and organization are skills that must be developed by preservice teachers through the educator preparation process.

Volumes of books have been written on classroom management tips and strategies. This section of Chapter 8 is not designed to add to those volumes. Instead, it will offer insight regarding underlying principles that support and guide a preservice teacher in earning students' respect. In classrooms where teachers are caring, firm, fair, and consistent, classroom management is not problematic.

Carefully read and contemplate the three simple precepts that comprise the "Classroom Management: Guiding Principles" document that follows:

Classroom Management

Guiding Principles

CARE   Students don't care how much you know, until they know how much you care.

Image © Monkey Business Images, 2013. Used under license from Shutterstock, Inc.

FAIR   Set standards that are fair, and be both firm and friendly when presenting and enforcing those standards.

Image © AWesleyFloyd, 2013. Used under license from Shutterstock, Inc.

CONSISTENT   **Draw a line (set boundaries) for student behavior . . . and hold students to that line.**

Image © AkbudakRimma, 2013. Used under license from Shutterstock, Inc.

 LET'S TALK

With a partner, share a recollection of one of your own K-12 classroom experiences that was rife with disorder and poor student behavior. Speculate as to which of the three aforementioned guiding principles was lacking.

THINK AND WRITE

Which of the three guiding principles will likely be the easiest for you to master? Which of the three guiding principles will likely be the most difficult for you to master? Explain.

EXERCISE: Teacher Interview

Briefly interview two classroom teachers: one experienced classroom teacher, and one who has recently entered the teaching profession. Ask the following questions, and type out brief notes that summarize each teacher's response:

1. Identify and explain your three most effective classroom management strategies.
2. Describe your most challenging classroom management experience, and speculate as to why you struggled to manage that situation.
3. Briefly review the "Classroom Management: Guiding Principles" document, and then share your initial reaction as to which guiding principle you most firmly support and what—if any—additional guidelines you would add to the list.

 LET'S TALK

In small groups, compare the responses of the new teachers. What—if any—common themes did you notice?

 LET'S TALK

In small groups, compare the responses of the experienced teachers. What—if any—common themes did you notice?

 THINK AND WRITE

Compose a brief essay comparing and contrasting the themes noted in the new teacher/experienced teacher interviews on classroom management.

FIELD OBSERVATIONS AND REFLECTIONS

Most actual learning of the practice of a profession takes place on the job.

(Sullivan, 2005, p. 198)

Undoubtedly, much of the professional knowledge that an effective teacher possesses is tacit knowledge that has developed through on-the-job experience. Therefore, to initiate the development of tacit knowledge in preservice teachers, teacher educators must intentionally and continuously create opportunities for students to learn the art and science of teaching in mentored classroom-teaching settings. Through intentionally structured observation experiences and numerous opportunities to reflect upon those experiences, preservice teachers will begin develop understanding of the role of a professional educator. By so doing, a preservice teacher's professional development will be richly enhanced through field experiences.

Upon entering a professional educator's classroom as a mentored guest, it is imperative that the preservice teacher recognizes that he or she is to humbly observe and reflect upon the experience. The preservice teacher's role is to gather data and learn—not to judge or critique the teachers, professional staff, or the learners.

In that spirit of humility, the following sample contract was written by one professor to prepare preservice teachers for field observations.

FIELD EXPERIENCE: MENTORED GUEST A BEHAVIOR CONTRACT

- I am entering this classroom as a mentored guest, and will conduct myself in a manner that is consistent with the high standards of professionalism and the NEA Code of Ethics.
- As a mentored guest, I will make every effort to avoid disruption to the teacher, the learners, and the classroom setting.
- I will observe the teacher and other school professionals through the "lens of a learner," considering with humility that I am not in a position to judge or critique others who I may encounter.
- I will not post or publish my observations or reflections on social media or any other public venue.
- I will not engage with learners—even when I feel compelled to be helpful—unless granted permission by the classroom teacher.
- If I observe disturbing behaviors or suspect a child may be in harm's way, I will immediately report these observations or suspicions to my college instructor.
- I will strive to make a positive impact on the members of the learning community in any way that I can.

_____   Date _____

Student's Signature

📝 THINK AND WRITE

What is your initial reaction to this behavior contract? What did you find to be most surprising? What did you find to be most helpful? Explain your answers.

📝 THINK AND WRITE

Imagine that you are a certified classroom teacher who is working diligently to manage a challenging group of students who have a wide range of abilities and behavioral challenges. You are rapidly approaching "test week," the week of administering state-mandated standardized tests, and you are feeling nervous that your students are not yet prepared. Imagine that, at the same time, you have been asked to allow preservice teachers to observe in your classroom. Reread the behavior contract through the eyes of the classroom teacher, and record any new thoughts that come to your mind while reading the contract.

LET'S TALK

With a partner or in a small group, share your reactions to the "Mentored Guest" Behavior Contract and your related "Think and Write." Speculate as to why an instructor would feel the need to place such a contract before preservice teachers.

THINK AND WRITE

Before beginning your guided field observations, compose a list of vows you will take as a mentored guest who is humbly entering a professional educator's classroom. Consider structuring it as a "Behavior Contract" that you would want preservice teachers to sign before they enter *your* classroom some day.

EXERCISES

The Field Experience Data Collection charts and Field Experience Strategy Collection Charts that follow are provided so that preservice teachers will engage in field observations with tremendous intentionality followed by thoughtful reflection. Complete these forms while observing a range of grade levels (elementary, middle, and secondary) in a variety of settings (rural, urban, and suburban) in both public and private schools.

Field Experience Observation Guide

OBJECTIVES

Within the context of several K-12 classrooms, the learner will

- observe and reflect upon the range and nature of student diversity within each classroom;
- identify the advantages and disadvantages of teaching at each level: elementary, middle, and secondary;

- begin to discern which grade level and content area are best suited to his or her personal characteristics;
- evaluate the effect of his or her professional decisions and actions on students and others in the learning community;
- observe and reflect on classroom teachers' strategies for encouraging active involvement of students and families;
- observe and reflect on effective communication techniques between teacher and students; and
- identify personnel, articulate their roles in the K-12 school system, and explain how collaboration among the personnel will advance student learning.

Field Experience Data/Reflections   Student Name: _____

School Name: _____   Date of Observation: _____

Grade Level Observed: _____   Content Areas You Observed: _____

Teacher's Name: _____

POPULATION DEMOGRAPHICS	POSITIVE PROFESSIONAL SKILLS AND DISPOSITIONS OBSERVED IN SCHOOL PERSONNEL
Classroom #1: _____	Professionalism
Total # of students: _____	
Males _____/Females _____	
% of students of majority race/ethnicity _____	
% of students of minority race/ethnicity _____	Oral communication
# of students with special needs _____	
_____% of students of higher SES	
_____% of students of average SES	
_____% of students of lower SES	Human interaction
Classroom #2: _____	
Total # of students: _____	
Males _____/Females _____	
% of students of majority race/ethnicity _____	Critical thinking
% of students of minority race/ethnicity _____	
# of students with special needs _____	
_____% of students of higher SES	
_____% of students of average SES	Ethical leadership
_____% of students of lower SES	
EVIDENCE OF COLLABORATION *(that advances student learning)*	How and to what extent your presence, professional decisions, and/or actions affected the students and others in the learning community...
Administrator/Office staff	POSITIVELY
Teacher's aides/Title I/Literacy coaches	
	NEGATIVELY
Volunteers	

ADVANTAGES OF TEACHING	DISADVANTAGES OF TEACHING
1. This grade level 2. In a school with similar student demographics	1. This grade level 2. In a school with similar student demographics
Questions to ask instructor and/or questions to raise during Panel Discussions:	Can you see yourself teaching at this grade level? Explain. Can you see yourself teaching in this (rural/urban/suburban) setting? Explain.

Complete one of the following tasks listed below:

- Briefly describe a lesson plan idea that you found to be particularly valuable.
- Describe something you learned about *yourself* as a result of this observation experience.

Strategy-Gathering Charts: Template and Sample

OBJECTIVES

Within the context of several K-12 classrooms, the learner will

- observe and reflect on a variety of classroom management strategies;
- recognize strategies and techniques of classroom organization conducive to effective teaching and learning;
- observe and reflect upon a variety of instructional (pedagogical) strategies in a range of K-12 settings;
- observe and reflect upon a variety of student assessment strategies;
- observe and reflect upon a variety of strategies conducive to reaching diverse learners; and
- observe and reflect upon a variety of strategies that facilitate collaboration among teacher, families, and community members.

"Strategy Collection" Chart

Intended Grade Level/Content Area: Eleventh grade/Spanish

Date and Name of School	Grade Level and Content Area	Management	Pedagogy	Collaboration	Diversity	Assessment	Strategy Name	Describe Strategy (either you actually observed or an educator described it)	Ways You Can Adapt It (to your intended grade level/content area(s))
10/25/08 Wilson elementary	Second grade	✓					Roll call by folder	During the beginning of class, one student is assigned the job of walking around the room and placing a folder on each desk where a student is absent. The teacher then glances around the room and marks the students absent who have a brightly colored folder on their desk.	I would reverse the idea and have each student pick up a folder with their name and "bell work." The folders left over would indicate which students were absent.
11/2/08 Ames middle school	Eighth grade Social studies					✓	Ticket out the door	For closure and assessment, the teacher asks students to write three reasons that the South had better trained soldiers in the Civil War. Students are dismissed as they hand that piece of paper to the teacher who stands by the door.	I would still use it to assess key learning, but I would have colored paper cut into quarters "ready to go" so that students were not searching for a sheet of paper at the end of class.

"Strategy Collection" Chart from Field Observations

Your Intended Grade Level for Certification:____

Student Name ____

Certification Area(s): ____

Date and Name of School	Grade Level and Content Area	Management	Pedagogy	Collaboration	Diversity	Assessment	Strategy Name (create a short and catchy name if it has none)	Describe Strategy (either you actually observed this strategy or an educator described the strategy to you)	Ways You Can Adapt It (to your grade level/content area(s); if you cannot adapt it, do not include it!)

Strategy Collection Chart RUBRIC   Name _____

_____ / _____ strategies are valid strategies   School Name _____

	4 PTS.	3 PTS.	2 PTS.	1 PT.	0 PTS.
NAME AND DESCRIPTION OF STRATEGY Names are clever and descriptive; strategies are adequately described	All	Nearly all	At least half	Some	None
CLASSIFICATION of strategies—accuracy	All	Nearly all	At least half	Some	None
ADAPTATION of strategies—*accurately and fully developed*	All	Nearly all	At least half	Some	None
FORMATTING of chart and EDITING of language	All	Nearly all	At least half	Some	None

Total: _____ / 16 pts.

Strategy Collection Chart RUBRIC   Name _____

_____ / _____ strategies are valid strategies   School Name _____

	4 PTS.	3 PTS.	2 PTS.	1 PT.	0 PTS.
NAME AND DESCRIPTION OF STRATEGY Names are clever and descriptive; strategies are adequately described	All	Nearly all	At least half	Some	None
CLASSIFICATION of strategies—accuracy	All	Nearly all	At least half	Some	None
ADAPTATION of strategies—*accurately and fully developed*	All	Nearly all	At least half	Some	None
FORMATTING of chart and EDITING of language	All	Nearly all	At least half	Some	None

Total: _____ / 16 pts.

DISPOSITIONS AND DOCUMENTATION

10
CHAPTER

You cannot consistently perform in a manner which is inconsistent with the way you see yourself.

Zig Ziglar

Professional dispositions are habits of thoughts and actions that emanate from professional attitudes, values, and beliefs. This definition has three critical components worthy of careful analysis:

1. Habits: By definition, a habit is *repetitive* behavior, a tendency; no single incident constitutes a habit.
2. Thinking and action: *Thinking* and *thought patterns*, though less distinguishable than actions, are also dispositional by nature.
3. Emanate from attitudes, values, and beliefs: *Beliefs* and *values* are the wellspring of behavior.

As this definition suggests, behavior is a manifestation of an individual's beliefs and values. The dispositions of a professional educator are demonstrated verbally and nonverbally through interactions with students, families, and other education stakeholders. Therefore, as preservice teachers engage in professional development, it is vitally important that each candidate self-assesses professional behaviors and reflects upon the values, attitudes, and beliefs underlying each.

OBJECTIVES

The learner will:

- examine the three-part definition of *professional disposition* as it is used in the field of education;
- recall the dispositions displayed by previous teachers who positively influenced the learner and speculate as to the underlying values, attitudes, and beliefs of those teachers;
- acquire a copy of the School of Education's expectations for teacher candidates' professional dispositions;
- articulate the necessity for professional dispositions to be evident in the behaviors of those who aspire to teach; and
- evaluate personal behaviors, skills, and dispositions so as to discern readiness to enter the teacher education program and teaching profession.

THINK AND WRITE

Reflect upon the most influential teachers that you have encountered in your educational experience. Identify at least three habits you observed in those teachers that contributed to the positive impact each made on your life. Speculate as to some of those teachers' underlying attitudes, values, and beliefs about students and learning.

LET'S TALK

In small groups, brainstorm two lists:

- List One: attitudes, values, and beliefs that you think teachers should have in common.
- List Two: professional behaviors that you think teachers should have in common.

Compare your group's lists with others. What are the commonalities among the lists?

WEBCONNECT

Search your institution's School of Education website to locate and download the list of Professional Dispositions that your program espouses. If a Professional Disposition form is not readily available, use the Professional Skills and Dispositions form included in this chapter as a reference.

EXERCISE

Complete a thoughtful self-assessment of your habits of action and mind using your program's Professional Dispositions form or the Professional Skills Dispositions form included in this chapter.

THINK AND WRITE

You have spent a considerable amount of time examining the professional dispositions of effective educators. Perhaps most important of all, you have engaged in self-assessment in this area. What have you discovered about yourself through this process? Make specific references to the Professional Dispositions form as you identify areas of strength and weakness.

Return your thoughts to the metaphor of the gears that figuratively comprise the engine of the effective teacher. The gears we have examined until now included oral communication skills, interpersonal skills, critical thinking skills, and professional knowledge. This chapter reveals the last of the gears: professional dispositions. Consider for a moment what would happen if an engine had only four of five gears in good working condition. Using the Forced Analogy technique explain the similarities between that engine and a teacher who has all of the skills of a professional educator, but is lacking in professional dispositions.

Based on your performances relative to the critical skills exercises and your self-assessments regarding the skills and dispositions of an effective teacher, do you consider teaching a good "fit" for you professionally? Explain. Be certain to make specific reference to your previous analysis of strengths and weaknesses on the Professional Skills and Dispositions inventory.

Note to Instructors

The following Professional Skills and Dispositions inventory is provided so that learners may self-assess their critical skills and dispositions as preservice teachers. I recommend that students complete the self-assessment regularly throughout the program so that they may track their progress and compose professional development plans in conjunction with the self-assessment and feedback they receive.

The remaining administrative forms in this chapter are to be used at your discretion. Identifying problematic behaviors and shaping positive dispositions can become a time-consuming task. Therefore, these forms are included so that instructors may efficiently and effectively communicate (and document) dispositional feedback to students. Perhaps just as important as communication and documentation is self-assessment. These forms provide students with the opportunity to self-report and reflect upon their behaviors that are incongruent with the dispositions of effective teachers.

Professional Skills and Dispositions

Student Name: _____

Standard Categories Target Indicators 1 = Needs Improvement 2 = Satisfactory NR = Not Observed/Rated

Standard Categories	Target Indicators	Self	Faculty	Comments
Communication Skills				
1. Listening	Listens purposefully and attentively. Uses active listening skills in conversations and class discussions.			
2. Speaking	Uses language and grammar appropriately. Conveys ideas clearly and effectively. Voice and elocution create and maintain interest.			
3. Writing	Writing is well organized and developed. Relatively error free, clear, with vocabulary appropriate for the audience.			
4. Reading Fluency	Demonstrates ability to read aloud accurately and fluently. Seldom mispronounces or uses words incorrectly.			
Critical Thinking Skills				
5. Comprehension	Constructs meaning and articulates key ideas from readings, lectures, conversations, and discussion.			
6. Analysis and Evaluation	Demonstrates proficient use of the elements of critical thinking when completing assigned readings.			
7. Problem Solving and Decision Making	Asks relevant questions. Provides reasoned evidence to support positions and opinions. Avoids logical fallacies.			
Human Interaction, Leadership, and Other Professional Dispositions				
8. Accepts Responsibility for Actions	Accepts consequences of decisions and actions without excuses. Seeks feedback and makes changes as necessary.			
9. Attendance and Preparation	Attendance and punctuality demonstrate high level of commitment. Absences are arranged in advance.			
10. Meets Deadlines	Assignments are submitted on time or early.			

11. Ethical Behavior	Honest. Truthful. Demonstrates personal integrity and academic integrity. Adheres to the NEA Code of Ethics for Professional Educators.				
12. Assignment Quality	Assignments show care and thoughtfulness, follow directions, and create a favorable impression.				
13. Classroom Participation	Contributes positively to class discussions and community building activities in class.				
14. Self-Confidence	Takes initiative, assumes leadership, responds to varied situations confidently.				
15. People Passion	Demonstrates passion for working with children and/or adolescents. Self-described "people person."				
16. Self-Awareness and Self-Regulation	Demonstrates awareness and understanding of feelings. Realistically self-assesses and effectively self-regulates behavior.				
17. Social Awareness	Has the "with-it-ness" to be aware of all others in the setting, acknowledge others' needs, and accurately interprets others' actions, questions, and responses.				
18. Appropriate Interactions	Relates to others in socially acceptable ways. Body language and vocalizations convey positivity, warmth, and empathy.				
19. Collaboration	Can play the role of either leader or equal member of a group and knows when it is appropriate to do so to accomplish goals of the group. Shares responsibility for group work and follows through on assignments.				
20. Diversity	Values diversity of personalities, needs, learning styles, ethnicities, cultures, and backgrounds.				
21. Professional Appearance	Neat and clean appearance appropriate to the setting, including proper "teaching attire" in classroom teaching situations.				

276

Portions of this survey were adapted from a Professional Skills and Dispositions document that is no longer used by the School of Education at Spring Arbor University.

Student Attendance / Dispositional Concern Documentation

Student Name: _____

Section #: _____   Lab or Classroom? _____   Date of Infraction: _____

Cause for Documentation (check all that apply):

_____ Failure to notify instructor in advance of absence

_____ Failure to notify instructor immediately following the absence (if a *dire* emergency prevented a call prior to class)

_____ Two or more absences (this includes excused   Number of absences to date?_____
absences also)

_____ Tardiness   Number to tardies to date? _____

_____ Failure to submit assignment(s) on time   Number of late assignments to date? _____

_____ Other: _____

Regarding attendance requirements, the course syllabus states (please quote):

Regarding homework completion, the course syllabus states (please quote):

I, _____, am aware that the previously noted behavior may significantly impact my course grade and as well as the evaluation of my professional skills and dispositions. Additionally, I am aware that pervasive and/or unremediated dispositional concerns may hamper my admission to the School of Education.

_____   Date _____
Student Signature / Student's Printed Name

_____   Date _____
Instructor's Signature

MISSING WORK Documentation

Student Name _____

Date _____

Please complete this form and submit it to the instructor before leaving class today.

Name(s) of Missing Assignment(s):

I am not submitting the homework that is due today because:

_____ I completed the assignment, but I did not bring it to class.

_____ I completed the assignment, but I did not submit it electronically before the deadline.

_____ I forgot to complete the assignment.

_____ I completed only a portion of the assignment.

_____ I chose not to complete the assignment.

_____ I completed the wrong assignment.

_____ I completed the assignment incorrectly.

_____ I missed a previous class and failed to review the Course Calendar regarding what was due today.

Please provide additional explanation if necessary.

Your instructor may choose to accept one assignment late (up to 24 hours beyond deadline) for partial credit.

Have you used this "GRACE CLAUSE for another assignment? _____

If no, would you like to submit this assignment for GRACE consideration? _____

[If multiple assignments are listed at the top, identify the ONE assignment for which you'd like GRACE.]

Pre-Arranged Absence: Request for *Excused* Absence

Student Name: _____   Date the Form was Submitted: _____

Course #: ____   Section #: ____   Date of Anticipated Absence: _____

Reason for Absence (check all that apply):

_____ Required university extracurricular event   _____ Required university course field trip

_____ Other (Please explain nature of absence.)

_____

_____

Regarding EXCUSED absence requirements, the course syllabus states:

Please check all that apply:

_____ If the date of absence falls upon a course date, I request that the instructor "waive" the participation requirement on that date so that I do not receive a zero in the grade book. I understand
that I *must* submit my homework PRIOR to this absence to receive the "waiver" on participation
points for that date.

_____ If the date of absence falls upon a field trip date, I agree to take the responsibility to contact
the host school and arrange an alternative date that I may observe PRIOR to the absence.

_____ If the date of absence falls upon an Independent Observation date, I agree to take the responsibility to contact the host school and arrange an alternative date that I may observe PRIOR
to the absence.

I, _____, have read the instructor's policies related to attendance and
homework submission related to absences, and I agree to comply with the directions listed above.

_____   Date _____
Student Signature / Student's Printed Name

_____   Date _____
Instructor Signature   Request Approved ____   Denied ____

Attendance Record   *Instructor Name* _____

                                                       Course # _____

<u>**M T W R F**</u>, _____
Day   Date

*******Please sign in and record the time. Thank you. This document is of great assistance for both instructor and students when evaluating professional behaviors and dispositions.   ***********

<u>Student Name</u>	<u>Time of Arrival</u>

PRESERVICE TEACHER—
CAREER PACKET

Courtesy of John Beck

These resources are designed to assist you in seeking employment within a school or any other teaching position. This career packet was compiled by Spring Arbor University's Career Planning and Placement office and is shared with permission.

These resources include:

- Resume Overview
- Creating an Education/Teaching Resume
- Action Verbs
- Resume Construction and Layout Checklist
- Cover Letter Basics

- Preparing for an Interview
- Favorite Questions Used During Teaching Interviews
- Sources for Job Leads
- Resume, Reference, and Heading Samples

RESUME OVERVIEW

Purpose of a Resume

A resume is used to show you have the knowledge, skills, and experience relevant to a *particular job and to entice the employer to interview you!*

Self-Assessment

In order to put together an effective resume, it is important to know your abilities, what skills you have developed, what values are important to you in a career, and what you can offer to an employer. The first step in preparing your resume is to think about yourself, your experiences, and your accomplishments.

Ask yourself these kinds of questions:

- What skills have I developed?
- What are my strengths?
- What have I accomplished?
- Why should someone hire me?

You may find it difficult at first to identify skills, until you think more deeply about your academic, social, work, and volunteer experiences. Students develop various skills in addition to those acquired through their major coursework. It is probably safe to assume many students develop organizational, communication, and interpersonal skills as a result of having to meet deadlines and communicate their ideas to a variety of people. As you review your experiences in this way you may soon discover additional skills.

When you have given sufficient thought to self-assessment, ask family and friends to assess your skills. Check their perceptions against your own and make any necessary adjustments in your personal career profile.

After analyzing your skills, accomplishments, strengths, and value to employers, you will discover the writing of your resume to be a much easier task.

CREATING AN EDUCATION/TEACHING RESUME

A resume must present information quickly, clearly, and in a way that makes your experience relevant to the position in question. That means that this resume should have information condensed down to its most powerful form.

Focus on the Following Areas

- Skills
- Accomplishments
- Student Teaching
- Experiences
- Leadership
- Academics

Identify Your Goal

You need to have a clear job target as you need to develop your resume. For example, the job objective in your resume should state your job specification with the keywords that are pertinent to your job profile.

Summary

You *could* summarize your strengths and key qualifications within the top half of the first page of the resume under a section called "Profile Summary," "Summary of Qualifications," or "Professional Profile" and using keywords that are pertinent to your occupational field choice in three to five bulleted statements.

Emphasize Your Accomplishments

Describe your basic job responsibilities or accomplishments using action verbs in short phrases or sentences. Show quantifiable results of your work that are relevant to the position you are seeking.

Include Keywords

Keywords are search terms used by employers to weed through resumes. Your resume should include these related keywords to ensure that it is found during the search.

Examples of keywords include job titles, degrees, certifications, professional organizations, and skills/areas of specialty. If a keyword has a widely used acronym, include both the spelled-out forms and abbreviated somewhere in your resume since an employer may use either during a search.

Resume Structure

You could research some resume templates online to find the right format for your needs. However, it is *not generally recommended to use a RESUME TEMPLATE* because they restrict you to their format and may not be how you want to communicate your skills, abilities, and experiences to the employer. Resumes should include the following sections:

- Your name and contact information
- Education
- Work and/or volunteer experience
- Skills and abilities

If you have just graduated from college or graduate school and you have little relevant work experience, you should place your educational qualifications at the top of your resume. If you have been working for a while and have a lot of relevant job experience, start your resume with your work experience and place your educational qualifications at the bottom.

Be sure that your resume is clear and concise. You do not have to be too descriptive, but make sure that you clearly express your accomplishments. Note the following example as the candidate states number and ages of young people, duration of work experience, and issues handled.

Work Experience (*Section Heading and Bullets Example*)

Antiochian Village Camp, Ligonier, PA Summers 2011, 2012

Camp Counselor

- Supervised the safety and well-being of 32 campers, ages 13–17, over four 2-week overnight sessions.
- Dealt with issues of homesickness, depression, suicide, grief, faith struggles, etc.

Quick Tips

- Be prepared in an interview to give further details and information on each part of your resume.
- Be as concrete as possible. For example, if you have experience running retreats, think of what worked and did not work as you were giving them.
- Have many friends look at your resume for corrections and comments.
- Make sure that your formatting and fonts are consistent throughout.
- DO NOT HAVE ANY SPELLING ERRORS.

ACTION VERBS AND KEY PHRASES

Use the following phrases and words to compose your resume statements. They convey involvement and accomplishments and make your resume more readable and effective.

Accomplished
Acted/functioned as
Administered
Advised
Amounting to a savings of
Analyzed/assessed
Arranged
Assigned to
Assisted with
Budgeted
Conducted
Consulted
Contracted/subcontracted
Coordinated
Counseled
Delegated
Delivered
Demonstrated
Developed
Direct/indirect control
Drafted

Edited
Established
Evaluated
Experience involved/included
Expertise and demonstrated skills
Extensive training/involvement
Familiar with
Formulated
Gathered
Handled
Honored as
Implemented
Improved
In charge of
Initiated
Innovation resulted in
Installed
Instructed
Instrumental in
Interaction with
Investigated

Knowledge of/experienced as
Liaison for/between
Maintained
Managed
More than [ ] years experience
Negotiated
Organized
Performed
Planned
Presented
Promoted to/from
Proven track record in
Provided technical assistance
Recipient of
Remained as
Resulted in
Sales quota accountability
Served/operated as
Skilled in
Specialized in
Successful in/at

RESUME CONSTRUCTION AND LAYOUT CHECKLIST

- Do not use a resume template—they are helpful but employers can see that you did not put much effort into creating your document.
- **Do not use words such as I, my, he, she, they, their, etc.**
- Use 8½ × 11 in. paper. The resume margins on the top to bottom should be ½ to 1 in. The left and right margins should be ½ to 1¼ in. Whatever you decide to use, it should be the same top–bottom and left–right.
- **Do not use the same action verb multiple times—mix it up** (see action verb list).
- Use the same font type in resume and letter—consistency is important!
- Your resume should be typed. *No exceptions.*
- Your resume should be well organized, concise, professional in style and appearance, and easy to read.
- Use a laser printer or ink jet set on fine/best quality. Photocopying your resume is not advised.
- Good-quality paper (cotton fiber 20-pound bond paper) should be used. Ivory and white are the most widely accepted colors of resume paper.
- Know the reader and what is acceptable in that career field before you make decisions regarding the paper, color, and design of your resume.
- **Stress accomplishments while being honest and accurate.**
- Spelling, grammatical, punctuation, or typographical errors are inexcusable. Have several people proofread your resume.

- Since you should use phrases instead of complete sentences, periods are not necessary.
- You may use some limited abbreviations on your resume (Example: PA, NJ, MI).
- Do not include personal information that is not related to the position you are applying for (e.g., race, age, sex, marital status, number of children, height, weight, and health status).
- Use caution also when including information related to political and/or religious affiliations.
- Your resume should be kept to one page if possible. *If you must go to two pages put your name and "Page 2" on the top left-hand side of the paper.*
- Do not use "References Available" at the end of the resume—often seen as filler.

ADDITIONAL RESOURCES FOR RESUME ASSISTANCE

Visit these websites for additional guidelines and samples for resumes and cover letters.

http://www.collegegrad.com
http://www.susanireland.com/resumeindex.htm
http://www.rileyguide.com/eresume.html
http://www.eresumes.com/

COVER LETTER BASICS

Once you have decided to apply for a job, you should send a cover letter and resume to the contact person for the job. Use the cover letter to introduce yourself and call attention to your enclosed resume. The well-written cover letter highlights aspects of your background and talents that best meet a school's needs. Also, always try to obtain the name of the person to whom the letter should be addressed.

First Paragraph

- Describe the position or title of the position you seek, for example, first-grade teacher, math teacher, or coach.
- If someone referred you, mention the person's name and explain your connection.

Second Paragraph

- Tailor to a particular job.
- Briefly explain the reason for your interest in teaching.
- Briefly and specifically summarize your most desirable qualifications that would meet their needs (consider bulleting three key qualifications).
- Explain how you intend to contribute to your student's development and the school.

Third Paragraph

- Add this only if there is additional information to amplify information in the second paragraph that is not in your resume or needs clarification (e.g., a special project you undertook at a previous job or in your community).

Closing Paragraph

- Thank the person for considering your candidacy and say that you are looking forward to meeting him or her and learning more about this opportunity.
- Remember to be truly interested, gracious, and respectful of their time.
- Be sure to follow through with any commitment you make.

PREPARING FOR AN INTERVIEW

The interview is often the primary vehicle through which hiring occurs. Highly qualified candidates may be turned down for teaching positions because they failed to communicate their talents and abilities. Similarly, underqualified candidates may be hired for, and ultimately fail in, teaching positions because they successfully oversold themselves. Preparing for an interview should help you and the organization make a good decision and, once the job begins, to actually do well.

- Research the school or organization.
  - Does it have a website?
  - Is it listed in a directory?
  - Google it!
  - Has it been featured in newspaper or magazine articles?
  - Do any of your contacts have any information for you?
- Research the job.
  - Analyze the job description, and match your experience, skills, interests, and abilities to the job.
  - Talk to people who have worked in similar positions. Your alumni association may help with locating contacts to network with.
- Prepare and anticipate questions. Answer the questions given to you. Try to avoid speaking in tangents.
- Practice your communication skills.
  - Present yourself in a positive manner.
  - Offer a firm handshake.
  - Speak clearly and effectively. Make sure that you are not chewing gum or sucking on hard candy during the interview.
  - Listen attentively and maintain eye contact.
  - Avoid the use of unnecessary verbal and nonverbal distractions.
- Dress appropriately.
- Be punctual.
- Turn off your cell phone.
- Write thank-you note(s) immediately after the interview to the person/people who interviewed you.

Ways to Practice Interviewing

- Have a friend or see your career services office to interview you.
- Conduct a mock interview with videotape.

- Conduct a mock interview with audiotape.
- Write out the answers to the interview questions.

Remember, preparation is meant to help you give organized and concise answers that reflect thought.

FAVORITE QUESTIONS USED DURING TEACHING INTERVIEWS

This list of questions would be an excellent resource for new teacher education graduates and alumni to use when preparing for interviews with school principals, superintendents, or personnel administrators.

Motivation and Personality

Tell me about yourself. What motivated you to enter teaching? What are your long-range career plans? Why have you selected education as a profession? Tell me about the teacher you would most like to emulate. Why did you decide to enter the field of education and your subject area in particular? Why did you want to become a teacher? What do you enjoy most about teaching?

Future Career Goals

What do you feel would be the most significant contribution you could make to our organization? How long would you plan to teach at this district? What is there about you that would cause a district to hire you over others? Are you interested in moving to this area? What are your future career goals—educational and professional? What do you expect to be doing 5 years from now?

Academic Preparation

What are your areas of certification? Tell me more about your other college coursework.

Student Teaching Experience

Describe your student teaching experience. Please tell me about your practice teaching and other work experiences with children. Did you enjoy your student teaching? Tell me about your class during student teaching. What was the highlight? What was the worst problem you had? How did you handle it? How did you generate the desire to learn in your students? Describe one activity or lesson that you were particularly proud of that you accomplished during your student teaching experience and would share. What adjectives would your students use to describe you?

Teaching Techniques and Style

What approaches or techniques work best for you in teaching? Explain your style of teaching—strategies, methodologies, techniques. What innovative ideas would you like to use in your classroom? Describe what I would see if I walked into your classroom while school was in session. What area would you like to strengthen? What are the traits of a good teacher? Please tell me about your best and worst teaching experience scenarios.

What do you feel are your greatest teaching strengths? What seem to be your greatest teaching weaknesses?

In what kind of work environment are you most comfortable? What lesson components do you include in your teaching? Do you believe in detailed lesson plans?

How do you accommodate individual differences? What experiences do you have with implementing individualization? What steps would you take to improve a student's self-concept? What techniques would you use to motivate students? How would you motivate the hard-to-reach child?

What is your philosophy of disciplining? What are your ideas about discipline? How do you teach reading and/or how do you affect good classroom management? What are your convictions regarding discipline? Should teachers paddle students?

How do you receive feedback, appropriate criticism? How will you appraise your teaching performance? How would you define teaching as a job? As a profession—How do you keep current in the field? Are you prepared to put in more hours than 8–5? Attend in-services?

Knowledge of the Employer

What do you think you could contribute to our school system? What do you know about our school district? Town? Why do you want to be a teacher in our district? What do you wish to contribute to our school and our children? Are you willing to relocate?

Hypothetical Questions

What would you do if: (a) You caught a student cheating? (b) A student never had his homework completed? (c) A student seemed to be an outcast in the class? (d) You knew a student had a very serious personal problem?

How will you go about meeting the needs of exceptional students? Describe the best teacher you have known. How would you respond to a situation like xyz?

How would you handle an incorrect oral answer? Do you view the role of the teacher as instructor or facilitator? What strategies do you use to evoke higher-order thinking?

How important is it for you as a teacher to assist in the development of a positive self-concept in students? How would you do this? What is your greatest strength as a teacher? What evidence can you share that students learn and respond to you better than most?

Explain those teaching strategies that have been most successful for you? Why? If money was unlimited, how would you improve education?

Structured Interviews

Some employers use structured interview formats (i.e., Ventures for Excellence—Teacher Selection, Teacher Perceiver Interview from Selection Research Inc., and Targeted Selection from Developmental Dimensions Inc. (DDI)). Situational-type questions are used (i.e., what would you do if . . . How would you . . .).

Some districts have designed their own interview formats covering mission, organization and planning, instruction, curriculum, evaluation, classroom management, and interpersonal skills.

BEST QUESTIONS ASKED BY JOB APPLICANTS DURING INTERVIEWS

Below is a list of some questions that could be very helpful when teacher education candidates are preparing for interviews with prospective employers.

General Topics

Why would I want to teach in your district? What does your school district offer that others do not or cannot? How might I help your school district? How would teachers (parents, others) describe your school district? What is the general pupil enrollment trend in your district (increasing, decreasing, or stable)? What is the financial status of your district? Does your district hire all first-year teachers?

Philosophy of Education

What is your district's philosophy of education? Do you believe all children can learn? How do teachers in your district accommodate and still assure success? What is your definition of a "quality" education? What is the mission (or major goals) of your school district?

Knowledge of Students

What percentage of high school graduates from your district go to college? What can I expect to learn from my students? What are your administrators doing for their students? What is the multiethnic mix of students in your district? What is the teacher/pupil ratio in your district? What are the multicultural needs of students?

Instructional Programs

How is your district improving classroom instruction? What curricular materials are available in your district? Where does your district want to be 5 or more years from now? What are the newest curricular changes in your district?

Anticipated Job Responsibilities

What are you seeking in the candidate you hire for this position? What do you expect from a teacher in the classroom? What are your administrators doing for their teachers?

Assistance for Beginning Teachers

What programs do you have for assisting first-year teachers? Does your school district have a mentor teacher program? If so, please describe it. What does your district do to insure that new teachers succeed? What support systems are available to a new teacher in your district?

Work Environment

What curriculum/tests do you use? Does your district allow creative teaching? How would you describe the classroom management/disciplining techniques used by teachers in your school district? How is technology being used in your district?

Teachers and Other Professionals

What could I learn from your teachers? What is the collegial relationship of teachers and others on your staff? How much support can I expect from the principal and parents? Will I get positive feedback from my supervisor?

Extracurricular Activities

What participation do you expect from a teacher in community and after-school activities? Is there a district policy regarding student activities scheduled on weekends so parents may participate?

Measures of Work Performance

How do you evaluate probationary teachers? What do you expect of teachers in your district? What are your observable standards? What relationship should exist between a teacher and his or her students? On what competencies should I focus during my first 6 months on the job? . . . first year?

School District Factors

How does this school view change? Do you support your faculty during opposition? What programs are offered to special education students?

Professional Development

What in-service staff development opportunities does your school district provide? Does your district encourage professional advancement? What colleges or universities are nearby, so I might complete a degree or improve my position? Does your district pay tuition assistance?

Community and Living Conditions

What housing is available in the community? What cultural activities are available in the community?

Salary and Benefits

(Note: According to surveyed employers, these are not good questions to ask at the first interview.) What is the starting salary for a beginning teacher with a bachelor's degree in your district? What is the job security of a new teacher in your district? What benefits are available to me other than salary in your district?

Interview Closure Questions

What additional preparation would I need to teach in your school district? Why would you hire another candidate for this position?

Based on your research, you may have many additional questions to add.

SOURCES OF JOB LEADS

For some people, the "perfect" job in a school or organization is open at the right time for them, and simply lands in their lap. For most people, however, a bunch of very human factors complicate finding that opportunity: for example, there are no jobs open in your home region; there is a job open but it will be a year or two until the school district is ready to commit a salary to it; the only jobs open are in teaching, but your gifts are working in a different subject area or age group. It will serve you well to do a good search for a teaching position, to find a good match with an open position and your unique abilities and talents.

Here are some sources of job leads and networking contacts:

- Family members and their friends.
- Online job-listing services accessible through the Internet (e.g., youthspecialities.com).
- Friends and their friends and relatives.
- Faculty and classmates where you attended school.
- University career services department.
- Networking with colleagues in your present organization and field.
- Alumni network from your school.
- Job postings organizations that have teaching positions.
- Your home church or pastor.
- Trade journals and newsletters.
- Directories.
- Professional association members.

Chronological Education Resume Sample

YOUR NAME

School Address	*Home Address*
0000 E. Main Street	000 South Austin Road
Spring Arbor, MI 49283	Elk, IL 50671
000-555-0000 Cell	000-555-0000 Home

EDUCATION

Bachelor of Arts, Spring Arbor University, Spring Arbor, MI   To be awarded May 20xx
Major: Spanish   Minor: French   Specialization: Secondary Education
- Participated in cross-cultural program to Spain.
- Cumulative GPA: 3.45/4.00.

CERTIFICATIONS

Michigan Secondary Provisional	To be awarded February 20xx
Christian Educational Leadership Endorsement	To be awarded June 20xx
CPR/First Aid Certification	Awarded January 20xx

TEACHING EXPERIENCE

Student Teacher, Public High School, Spring Arbor, MI   March–June 20xx
- Assumed full responsibility for two French I classes, one French II class, and two Spanish I classes.
- Presented culture unit on art and music of Spain.
- Designed and supervised cooking project, exploring cuisine of French-speaking countries around the world.

Field Experience, Eastmoor Middle School, Hilliard, OH   January–March 20xx
  • Developed long-range unit and lesson planning skills for beginning French and Spanish classes.
  • Assisted with annual Spanish culture food fair.
  • Aided teacher in general classroom activities.

Field Experience, Bolton Hollow Middle School, Hilliard, OH   September–December 20xx
  • Observed Spanish and French classes.
  • Tutored five students with introductory French.
  • Supervised Spanish Club's design of hallway display for parent Open House.

Camp Counselor and Instructor, Camp Horizons, Roanoke, VA   June–August 20xx
  • Taught beginning Spanish and canoeing.
  • Organized multicultural festival.

RELATED EXPERIENCE

Conversation Partner for International students, Spring Arbor University   Fall 20xx–Spring 20xx
Waitress, Café Francais, Jackson, MI   January–June 20xx
Student Office Worker, Language Department,
Spring Arbor University   September 20xx– May20xx
Clerk, Sarazin Imports, Chicago, IL   Summer 20xx

Functional Education Resume Sample

YOUR NAME

Current Address:	**Permanent Address:**
Address	Address
City, State, Zip Code	City, State, Zip Code
Phone Number	Phone Number
E-mail address	E-mail address

OBJECTIVE

To obtain an elementary teaching position utilizing my communicational, instructional, organizational, and classroom management skills.

EDUCATION

Bachelor of Arts, Spring Arbor University, Spring Arbor, MI   To be awarded 5/200X
Major: Early Childhood Education
  • Cumulative GPA: 3.4/4.0, Major GPA 3.78/4.00.
  • Dean's List (2 semesters) and received YMCA Academic Scholarship.

CERTIFICATION

Michigan Elementary Education Certificate	To be awarded 2/200X
Water Safety Instruction Certification	Awarded 2/200X
CPR Certification	Awarded 2/200X

TEACHING EXPERIENCE

- Taught, assisted, and observed first and fifth graders in resource classroom.
- Adapted and modified instruction to suit learning styles of students.
- Planned and prepared daily lesson plans and materials.
- Created a behavior management plan and assisted in assessment of student performance.
- Developed and implemented individual lesson plans for each student.
- Attended district meetings and team meetings.
- Instructed class of 18 for 2 weeks in teacher's absence.
- Taught, assisted, and observed second-grade students in all content areas.
- Motivated students through enthusiastic teaching and creative lessons.
- Encouraged student participation by creating supportive and welcoming classroom environment.
- Attended second-grade team meetings, staff meetings, and parent conferences.

TEACHING HISTORY

Student Teacher, C. C. Mason Elementary School, Homer, MI	2/200X–3/200X
Student Teacher, Public Elementary School, Horton, MI	1/200X–2/200X

CAREER-RELATED EXPERIENCE

Camp Counselor, Lochearn Camp for Girls, Post Mills, VT	6/200X–8/200X

- Co-organized youth education and social activities.
- Instructed swimming daily and communicated techniques with campers.
- Supervised 30+ adolescent girls with cabin and kitchen maintenance.
- Established written communication with parents.

Swimming Instructor, Abilene YMCA, Abilene, TX	Summers 200X, 200X, 200X

- Instructed multiple levels of swimming.
- Developed daily lesson plans and communicated with parents.

Combination—Chronological Education Resume Sample

YOUR NAME

Current: 0000 E. Main Street, Spring Arbor, MI 49283   000-555-0000
Permanent: 000 South Austin Road, Elk, IL 50671   yourname@email.com

PROFILE SUMMARY

- Foreign language skills include fluency in Spanish and conversational French.
- Cross-cultural experiences include Romania, Italy, Spain, and France.
- Dedication to task, organization, and time management.
- Active interest in reading, music, travel, and the outdoors.

EDUCATION

Bachelor of Arts, Spring Arbor University, Spring Arbor, MI   To be awarded May 20xx
Major: English   Specialization: Elementary Education
- Participated in cross-cultural program to Spain.
- Cumulative GPA: 3.45/4.00.

CERTIFICATIONS

Michigan Elementary Provisional   To be awarded February 20xx
Special Education Endorsement   To be awarded June 20xx
CPR/First-Aid Certification   Awarded January 20xx

TEACHING EXPERIENCE

Student Teacher, Public High School, Spring Arbor, MI   March–June 20xx
- Assumed full responsibility for two French I classes, one French II class, and two Spanish I classes.
- Presented culture unit on art and music of Spain.
- Designed and supervised cooking project, exploring cuisine of French-speaking countries around the world.

Field Experience, Eastmoor Middle School, Hilliard, OH   January–March 20xx
- Developed long-range unit and lesson planning skills for beginning French and Spanish classes.
- Assisted with annual Spanish culture food fair.
- Aided teacher in general classroom activities.

Field Experience, Bolton Hollow Middle School, Hilliard, OH   September–December 20xx
- Observed Spanish and French classes.
- Tutored five students with introductory French.
- Supervised Spanish Club's design of hallway display for parent Open House.

Camp Counselor and Instructor, Camp Horizons, Roanoke, VA   June–August 20xx
- Taught beginning Spanish and canoeing.
- Organized multicultural festival.

RELATED EXPERIENCE

Conversation Partner for International Students, Spring Arbor University   Fall 20xx–Spring 20xx
Waitress, Café Francais, Jackson, MI   January–June 20xx
Student Office Worker, Language Department,
Spring Arbor University   September 20xx–May20xx
Clerk, Sarazin Imports, Chicago, IL   Summer 20xx

Combination—Functional Education Resume Sample

YOUR NAME

106 East Main Street, Spring Arbor, MI 49283   (517) 000-0000   youremail@arbor.edu

OBJECTIVE

To obtain an elementary teaching position utilizing my communicational, instructional, organizational, and classroom management skills.

PROFILE SUMMARY

- Foreign language skills include fluency in Spanish and conversational French.
- Cross-cultural experiences include Romania, Italy, Spain, and France.
- Dedication to task, organization, and time management.
- Active interest in reading, music, travel, and the outdoors.

EDUCATION

Bachelor of Arts, Spring Arbor University, Spring Arbor, MI   To be awarded 5/200X
Major: Early Childhood Education
- Cumulative GPA: 3.4/4.0, Major GPA 3.78/4.00.
- Dean's List (two semesters) and received YMCA Academic Scholarship.

CERTIFICATION

Michigan Elementary Education Certificate   To be awarded 2/200X
Water Safety Instruction Certification   Awarded 2/200X
CPR Certification   Awarded 2/200X

TEACHING EXPERIENCE

- Taught, assisted, and observed first and fifth graders in resource classroom.
- Adapted and modified instruction to suit learning styles of students.
- Planned and prepared daily lesson plans and materials.
- Created a behavior management plan and assisted in assessment of student performance.
- Developed and implemented individual lesson plans for each student.
- Attended district meetings and team meetings.
- Instructed class of 18 for 2 weeks in teacher's absence.
- Taught, assisted, and observed second-grade students in all content areas.
- Motivated students through enthusiastic teaching and creative lessons.
- Encouraged student participation by creating supportive and welcoming classroom environment.
- Attended second-grade team meetings, staff meetings, and parent conferences.

TEACHING HISTORY

Student Teacher, C. C. Mason Elementary School, Homer, MI   2/200X–3/200X
Student Teacher, Public Elementary School, Horton, MI   1/200X–2/200X

CAREER RELATED EXPERIENCE

Camp Counselor, Lochearn Camp for Girls, Post Mills, VT   6/200X–8/200X
- Co-organized youth education and social activities.
- Instructed swimming daily and communicated techniques with campers.
- Supervised 30+ adolescent girls with cabin and kitchen maintenance.
- Established written communication with parents.

Swimming Instructor, Abilene YMCA, Abilene, TX   Summers 200X, 200X, 200X
- Instructed multiple levels of swimming.
- Developed daily lesson plans and communicated with parents.

Education Reference Page Sample

YOUR NAME

School Address	*Home Address*
0000 E. Main Street	000 South Austin Road
Spring Arbor, MI 49283	Elk, IL 50671
000-555-0000 Cell	000-555-0000 Home

REFERENCES

Name
Title, Employer
Mailing address
City, St ZIP
E-mail
Phone #

Name
Title, Employer
Mailing address
City, St ZIP
E-mail
Phone #

You should have a minimum of three people listed as professional references. These could be two academic and one previous employer or supervisor. Remember that these are not personal references.

Format—this document should mirror your resume.

Sample Resume Headings

YOUR NAME

106 East Main Street, Spring Arbor, MI 49283	(517) 000-0000	youremail@arbor.edu

YOUR NAME

0000 Pheasant Run Dr, Anywhere, MI 00000	517.000.0000	yourname@yahoo.com

YOUR NAME

Current Address:	*Permanent Address:*
Address	Address
City, State, Zip Code	City, State, Zip Code
Phone Number	Phone Number
E-mail address	E-mail address

References

Berliner, D. C. (2005). The near impossibility of testing for teacher quality. *Journal of Teacher Education, 56*(3), 205–213.

Byrnes, D., Kiger, G., & Shechtman, Z. (2003). Evaluating the use of group interviews to select students into teacher-education programs. *Journal of Teacher Education, 54*(2), 163–173.

Critical Thinking vs. Reflective Thinking. http://www.hawaii.edu/intlrel/pols382/Reflective%20 Thinking%20-%20UH/reflection.html downloaded March 15, 2014.

Denner, P. R., Salzman, S. A., & Newsome, J. D. (2001). Selecting the qualified: A standards-based teacher education admission process. *Journal of Personnel Evaluation in Education, 15*(3), 165–180.

Dybdahl, C. S., Shaw, D. G., & Edwards, D. (1997). Teacher testing: Reason or rhetoric. *Journal of Research and Development in Education, 30*(4), 248–254.

Fallon, M., & Ackley, B. (2003, April). *Standards for admission to teacher education programs.* Paper presented at the Annual Meeting of the American Educational Research Association. Chicago, IL.

Freiberg, H. J. (2002). Essential skills for new teachers. *Redesigning Professional Development, 59*(6), 56–60.

Guarino, G. M., Santibanez, L., & Daley, G. (2006). Teacher recruitment and retention: A review of the recent empirical literature. *Review of Educational Research, 76*(2), 173–208.

Ingles, S. (2010). A study of the Group Assessment Procedure for the Selection of Teacher Education Candidates at a Small, Private University in the Midwest, Unpublished doctoral dissertation, Capella University, Minneapolis, MN.

Petersen, G., & Speaker, K. (1996, February). *Bottom half of the pool: Who is admitted to teacher education?* Paper presented at the Annual Meeting of the Eastern Educational Research Association. Boston, MA.

Shechtman, Z. (1983). Validating a group interview procedure for the selection of teacher-education candidates in Israel. Unpublished doctoral dissertation, American University, Washington, DC.

Shechtman, Z. (1991). A revised group assessment procedure for predicting initial teaching success. *Educational and Psychological Measurement, 51*, 963–974.

Shechtman, Z., & Godfried, L. (1993). Assessing the performance and personal traits of teacher education students by a Group Assessment Procedure. *Journal of Teacher Education, 44*(2), 130–138.

Shechtman, Z., & Sansbury, D. (1989). Validation of a group assessment procedure for the selection of teacher-education candidates. *Educational and Psychological Measurement, 49*(3), 653–661.

Zimpher, N. L., & Howey, K. R. (1992). Policy and practice toward the improvement of teacher education: An analysis of issues from recruitment to continuing professional development with recommendations. Oak Brook, IL: North Central Education Lab.

Zufel, J. & Rasinski, T.V. (1989). Training teachers to attend to their students' oral reading fluency. *Theory into Practice, 30*(3), 214.

CPSIA information can be obtained
at www.ICGtesting.com
Printed in the USA
LVHW06s0623180818
587140LV00004B/11/P